CONVERSATIONS WITH

NORTH SEA OIL MOGULS

CONVERSATIONS WITH

NORTH SEA OIL MOGULS

JEREMY CRESSWELL

JURIDICAL

Juridical Ltd
Riverside House
Riverside Drive
Aberdeen AB11 7LH

First published 2005

ISBN 0 9550827 0 6

Typeset by Waverley Typesetters, Little Walsingham, Norfolk
Printed and bound by
Bercker Graphischer Betrieb GmbH & Co., Germany

Visit Juridical Ltd at www.juridical.co.uk

CONTENTS

FOREWORD

Jeremy Cresswell has written a special and noteworthy tribute to some of the heroes responsible for making the North Sea the last frontier of fresh oil supplies. He describes them as "Moguls". I use the term heroes because of the importance the North Sea had in creating what could possibly become the final great new horizon for oil.

My career as an energy investment banker was just beginning as North Sea oil was first discovered at the end of 1969. Prior to the "North Sea Oil Adventure", commercially developable offshore oil was deemed to be achievable only if found in shallow and benign waters.

Until the age of North Sea giants, when Ekofisk, Brent, Forties, Statfjord and others were discovered and developed, the big offshore arenas were all located in the first 40 miles off Louisiana and Texas, Lake Maracaibo in Venezuela, the shallow parts of the Persian Gulf, the Nigerian Delta and shallow waters scattered around South East Asia. The only offshore "frontier" at the end of the 1960s was the promise of California's Santa Barbara channel in over 250 feet of water but only a few miles from shore.

At the end of 1969, for anyone to imagine that oil would end up being produced throughout the most bitter of North Sea winters or in water depths up to 10,000 feet in the Gulf of Mexico, and some 200 miles from land, would have challenged even the imagination of Jules Verne.

By focusing on a select group of entrepreneurs whom Cresswell calls "North Sea Moguls", he highlights the true pioneers responsible for opening up the last great oil basin found in the past four decades. Cresswell also pays special tribute to these "moguls" because none were knighted British gentry, or senior executives of Big Oil. Instead, these North Sea corporate heroes were simply a collection of rugged entrepreneurs whose vision and willingness to tackle risks was why the North Sea challenge finally succeeded. These risk-takers knew how to take genuine risks.

When I read these great tributes to genuine "moguls" or "heroes", it caused me to think back to some of the other "North Sea Moguls" I had the pleasure of knowing, like Laddie Handleman, founder of Oceaneering, whose drive to ensure the safety of men working at unlimited water depths earned him the title of "Thomas Edison of deepwater energy". Or, colourful folks like Nolty J. Theriot of Golden Meadow, Louisiana, who sent his tough anchor-handling tug boats and crews to Great Yarmouth and Aberdeen to make sure the complex construction barges owned by Brown & Root and McDermott could operate as efficiently in the deep North Sea as they had in the shallow waters of the Gulf of Mexico. Or, the Heeremas of Holland who found ways to lift weights off the water unheard of before.

The North Sea ultimately became the true "Silicon Valley of deepwater technology". The Moguls responsible for this miracle ought to be appropriately honoured, which this book does in grand style.

Matthew R. Simmons
Houston
July 2005

INTRODUCTION

I am one of those people who loves a challenge so, when I was asked if I would tackle this book, doubts were instantly cast to one side and I grasped the opportunity.

After all, having written about the upstream oil and gas industry intensively since 1989, nearly all of it as a member of staff at Britain's oldest daily newspaper, Aberdeen's famous *The Press and Journal*, something must have rubbed off on me along the way.

Over the intervening 16 years I have been lucky enough to rub shoulders with literally hundreds of decision-makers in this astonishing industry. Many have been very generous with their time, including those who lead Big Oil, as oil majors such as BP, ExxonMobil and Shell are often colloquially referred to, and contracting majors such as Halliburton and Weatherford.

Indeed, outstanding in that regard is BP supremo John Browne. I first interviewed him in a Houston hotel penthouse suite in 1991 having lost my voice – he ordered a herbal tea for me. Then there is Chevron vice-chairman Peter Robertson. I finally met him earlier this year and learned that he was a Scot; moreover, his mother was Peterhead-born. I must not overlook Robert E. (Bob) Rose, a North Sea drilling pioneer who, before retiring in 2004, climbed the ladder to become chairman and president of the largest drilling corporation in the US – GlobalSantaFe. His wisdom has proved invaluable to me over the past decade at least. And last year I flew to Moscow to meet the then top team at Yukos, the beleaguered Russian oil major whose CEO Mikhail Khordokovsky had been imprisoned for alleged fraud and tax evasion at the order of President Vladimir Putin pending trial. He has since been found guilty in the Moscow courts on multiple counts and jailed for nine years. Part of that particular trip included flying to Western Siberia aboard Khordokovsky's private jet, a leather-upholstered TU134 airliner complete with bearskin bedecked double bed, to see Yukos production operations.

Though I have travelled fairly widely, most of my work has inevitably been focused on the North Sea. After all, this energy province remains one of the leading oil- and gas-producing regions in the world, even though it is now several years past its peak, especially in the British sector (otherwise known as the UK Continental Shelf).

Over the years hardly a week has gone by, even during vacations, without someone in the industry phoning me to impart good, but occasionally bad, news or because they want to meet and bounce a few thoughts around, sound me out, ask for my views (heaven knows why), often in confidence. I have sometimes been absolutely astonished at just who has been willing to share some very personal opinions on and concerns about the oil and gas industry and especially the plight of the UK energy supply chain, even to the point of being downright subversive.

Long ago in another "life" I learned to build Chinese walls. Today, the archive of confidences imparted since late 1989 is so large that I carry a veritable Kew Gardens maze of walls around in my mind. I cannot write about them, at least not directly, as that would represent a betrayal of trust.

I have, of course, ruffled a few feathers along the way. In that I count myself lucky as no journalist worth his or her salt can cruise through life avoiding controversy, having rows and, occasionally, making mistakes. I've certainly experienced my fair share of all three – in the case of mistakes, all too publicly. Arguably the worst period in terms of criticism for what I have written as a P&J staffer was during the global oil downturn of late 1997 through early 1999 when the price of a barrel of crude slumped to barely $8, briefly, during the dark days of November 1998. We (as a newspaper and me in particular) were accused time and again of talking down the North Sea. Reality was that it was the industry itself that held the spade – especially oil company bosses – and was doing a brilliant job of burying itself amid a huge amount of "woe are we" rhetoric. It was a gruesome time and one that I would rather not go through again.

Right now, the oil and gas industry is five years into a period of sustained good to excellent oil prices, with benchmark West Texas and Brent crudes riding above $50 per barrel for much of the current year (2005) to date (June) and every prospect of staying thereabouts at least until next year and perhaps far longer given that supply and demand are now so finely balanced, with little spare production capacity worldwide and, arguably, zero spare refining capacity. Gas prices are incredible – $80 per barrel oil equivalent here in Britain as I write this.

Now should be a fantastic time for the North Sea. I would go so far as to say that the province should be experiencing a prolonged "Indian summer", with traditional operators (oil companies) furiously harvesting cash cow assets – fields such as Brent, Britannia, Cormorant, Foinaven, Magnus, North Alwyn/Dunbar and Schiehallion – while new generation, lean "independents" sweep up hundreds of small oil and gas accumulations and occasionally get lucky with a really big oil strike, such as Canadian group Encanca did with Buzzard in June 2001.

It should also be a fabulous time for the UK oil and gas supply chain to trade on the back of some 35 years of North Sea experience and internationalise in a way that perhaps no other industry in these islands is capable of. For sure, there are plenty of very high calibre leaders out there and I know many of them personally. Most run SMEs; a lucky few head listed companies of substance. Some such people include: Douglas Craig, managing director of the roughly £100 million turnover family-owned Craig Group; Tom Smith, founder of Nessco and ceaseless campaigner on behalf of the Scottish energy SME community; Melfort Campbell, MD of IMES, who is also deputy chairman at CBI Scotland; Richard Selwa, founder/CEO at multi-faceted Vienco, which is both a service group and aspiring oil company; and John Ray, founder of Rigblast, who stepped back for a number of years but is back again as chairman of RBGltd, a £52 million three-way merger involving Rigblast, Fallsky and Mach-Ten Offshore. Then there is Ken Fraser, founder/chairman of specialist drilling company Norwell which celebrated its 15th year in business earlier this year to the thunder of Bhangra drummers at Aberdeen's smartest hotel; Syd Fudge, now retired from the heavy end of the business – production platform construction – but who keeps busy as a non-executive director sitting on the boards of seven energy SMEs; Mike Salter, chief operating officer at FTSE-listed Abbot Group; Bob Lyons of the fast-growing well management group Peak; and Mel Fitzgerald, for long a Halliburton senior and today CEO of underwater contracting group Subsea 7.

And not overlooking Steve Remp, who has been to hell and back again twice over with Ramco, initially a service company that he set up in the 1980s and, today, a listed cross between an exploration and production outfit and services provider. He rode Ramco's share price past £10 in 1997 on the back of huge promise in the oil-rich Caspian Sea. But Lady Luck faded away, the group's share price slumped and never recovered. Last winter it crashed to just over 20p because of the perceived virtual failure of an offshore Ireland gasfield development and an attempted rescue buy-out fell through. As if the foregoing isn't enough, Remp has been engaged in a battle with cancer.

In the Aberdeen area alone, there are some 900 companies engaged in servicing the needs of oil companies, variously North Sea and/or internationally. UK-wide, upstream oil and gas accounts for around 260,000 jobs.

What makes the people in this industry tick? What are the qualities that enable them to succeed in an industry that is, for the purpose of this book, roughly 35 years old? Then how do they find the inspiration and money to take the risk and, having taken the plunge, avoid getting complacent and opting for a lifestyle business that delivers a smart house up Aberdeen's North Deeside Road (one of the wealthiest corners of Britain), a place in the sun, lifetime membership of a couple of golf clubs and ample money invested or in the bank to live out the remainder of their lives, with a fat inheritance for their offspring?

There appears to be a broad pattern though this has yet to be confirmed through systematic research. Many start out in life working variously for an oil major, or a big-brand service company such as Baker Hughes, Halliburton or Schlumberger. Given that the average age in the UK offshore industry is now 53 – it's much the same in the US – that means most workers and bosses are post-1945 "baby-boomers" and it would seem that many left school to go straight into a job and work their way up, rather than pursue a degree at university. For some, the higher education experience has come later in life. Indeed, I read for my MBA at Aberdeen Business School (The Robert Gordon University) in the mid-1990s alongside a cadre of such individuals. Roughly around the age range 30–40, many seem to get frustrated and want to make a life for themselves, either because they have hit the career path buffers, or they're fed up with being a tiny cog in a very large machine. So they leave, usually with ample money in the bank, house paid for and a BMW or Mercedes in the driveway, and try the entrepreneurship game.

Then there are those who had no choice, slung out of oil companies especially as a result of the 1986 oil price crash and subsequent late 1990s downturn, but generally with fat pay-offs. Indeed, I've often said that, if I wanted to be paid off by any company, let it be a large oil corporation.

Most have qualifications, but these are nearly always directly linked with their profession. In this industry that generally means being a petroleum engineer, mechanical engineer, geologist and so-forth. It seems that very few have formal management qualifications, though many have been put through a short course of one form or another by their employers so that they can better handle teams of people assigned to them for projects, maintenance programmes or whatever.

As often as not, what gives many such individuals known to me the confidence to strike out on their own is the sight of their peers making their fortune, though the road is littered with quiet failures because their strategy was wrong or, all too often, there was no strategy. That said, I have paid very close attention to the public notices of *The Press and Journal* since the late 1990s slump that saw something like 100,000 oil- and gas-related jobs in Britain evaporate. Remarkably, there were very few company failures during that downturn, or in the year following said downturn, when one might legitimately have expected fall-out from oil company cost-cutting. I, and many others, thought that there would be myriad failures during that period. We were wrong. I counted fewer than a handful of collapses where corporate undertakers were called in to salvage what they could from the remains. If anything, there are more company collapses today than during that period. What happened instead was that large service companies appear to have picked up a significant number of struggling SMEs, generally quietly, because they offered a valuable, differentiated service of worth, and/or they had intellectual property that could be exploited. Some were rescued in well-publicised merger or takeover transactions involving the Aberdeen arm of Houston energy bankers Simmons & Company International, or the oil and gas unit of venture capital provider 3i and sometimes others.

So what is the purpose of this book? It is to tell how a select group of individuals made it to the top of the oil and gas tree. They tell their own stories. Some are what one would broadly class as entrepreneurs, others are company people who have made a real mark within their respective organisations. Just one is a serial entrepreneur, though this is complicated by the fact that the individual concerned does not see himself that way even though he is among the most successful that Scotland and, more particularly, the North Sea oil and gas industry, has ever generated.

What follows is a series of ten profiles – the result of one-to-one conversations and written very much in the style of "From the Boardroom", a regular feature of *The Press and Journal Energy Monthly*, of which I am editor. None are women, which is a great pity: they are like hen's teeth in the UK oil and gas industry, both within oil companies and the supply chain. Eight are drawn from the supply chain, one is the head of a unique hybrid organisation and the tenth is the founder/president of a new generation exploration independent, of the kind that the UK energy supply chain is increasingly coming face-to-face with. In a sense, the last is the joker in the pack.

The ten profiles are:

Jim Atack, MD, Petrofac Production Services

Neil Bruce, oil and gas MD, AMEC

The four Dreelan brothers of Qserv

Tom Ehret, CEO, Stolt Offshore

John Kennedy, chairman, Vetco International

Larry Kinch, chairman, Energy Development Partners

Richard Marsh, MD, Tritech International

Arthur Millholland, president/CEO, Oilexco

Jimmy Milne, chairman/MD, Balmoral Group

Sir Ian Wood, chairman/CEO, John Wood Group; chairman JW Holdings

These men represent an intriguing cross-section of enterprise – from modest SME to the UK's largest energy service blue chips, to one of the world's leading subsea contracting groups, to a cross between a service company, oil company and investment house, to a curious oil minnow with links into Iraq. Three of the above – Richard Marsh, Jimmy Milne and Sir Ian Wood – hold honorary Doctorates. The companies collectively hold a substantial number of awards; indeed, tiny Tritech has two Queen's Awards for Enterprise, plus the Millennium Prize for a Scottish SME and the only double win in the Scottish Offshore Achievement Awards. AMEC and Wood Group also hold Queen's Awards.

The final part of this book pulls together the common characteristics and themes that emerge from the profiles. This book is not a deep probe into every nook and cranny of the individual styles; that is for others, and business school libraries are full of such titles anyway. It is the writer's opinion and, as it turns out, the common sentiment of those profiled, that most management books are far more complicated than they ought to be. (Having been obliged to work my way through such material in the past, I feel justified in making the comment.) The accent is on simplicity and the hope is that if it helps anyone – student or businessperson – think a little more deeply about their aspirations or their approach in the corporate world, then this book is doing its job.

1 JIM ATACK

UNDERSTATED MOGUL

JIM ATACK

Name	Jim Atack
Company	Petrofac Facilities Management
Company turnover	$400 m
Current position	Managing Director
Place of birth	Nottingham, England
Education	BSc Civil Engineering (Loughborough), SM Offshore Engineering (MIT)
First job	Motorway Construction
Best business decision	Joining Petrofac and buying Google shares
Worst business decision	I have a selective memory ... can't think of one, at least that I'd like to share
Which company in the upstream oil and gas industry do you admire and why?	I'm very keen on the clutch of new-start oil companies in the North Sea; they all started off in a difficult environment with strong management teams and oodles of confidence. Their current market caps demonstrate their terrific achievement in just a few short years
Biggest dislike of the industry	The oil industry tends to cry "Wolf" every time the oil price takes a hit; sadly people believe us ... and leave/don't join the industry. Meanwhile it gets bigger every year ... and we need more people to join up
Advice to anyone considering a career in the oil industry	Do your homework, understand the issues, make your commitments, know what you want to do, have an opinion
What do you think of management gurus?	I'm not sure that I've ever met one, although I've heard that there are a lot out there, and seen some books at the airport. I'd probably put Robert Townsend (ex CEO of AVIS) forward as an alternative to a "Guru" (Author of *Up the Organisation*). I think Dilbert has a lot to contribute, too
Favourite pastime	Building Projects, Gardens, Landscaping
Favourite book	Le Carre - *Tinker, Tailor, Soldier, Spy* - there's a new twist every time you pick it up
Who or what is your inspiration?	I tend to seek inspiration and ideas from lots of people, rather than look for a formula for success
Any further ambitions?	Take our North Sea Service Operator model into a much larger international context
Favourite quote/saying	If it ain't broke; break it

JIM ATACK

UNDERSTATED MOGUL

Jim Atack heads the supply chain company that has done more in the past decade than perhaps any other to change the contracting face of the UK North Sea – Petrofac Facilities Management, originally Atlantic Power.

This understated individual stands out in his own right and is certainly re-membered by the delegates at an oil industry function for daring to say that, whereas operating oil companies had their preferred contractors, Petrofac had its preferred operators. It was a quiet warning to oil companies to treat their supply chain with respect.

Way back in his teens, it would have been all too easy to dismiss Atack as unpromising future management material. He had been working on construction sites then building the new motorways after leaving school aged 16, with no clear plans for his future. It was a rough, tough, hire-and-fire world and getting work generally meant convincing the site foreman that you could do the job.

"Leaving school early put me out into the world; I learned a lot by working on construction projects. I had little schooling, and was a very young person in a very adult world and I made my own way," says Atack, suggesting that the basis of his management skills today may stem from that period.

"You don't act rough and tough when learning how to hire and fire people, especially if you're five feet eight inches. What you do learn is how to manage those people who are rough and tough and six foot four and have other ideas about what might happen. You have to use the tools at your disposal and, for me, getting violent and physical were not options.

"I worked in construction for four or five years, and this allowed me to shape my future. When you find your own way, I think it makes you more determined and much more enthusiastic to follow your goals. Working on the early UK motorway construction – I was on the M3 and M4 – was a very demanding, but hugely formative, period.

"But I quickly realised that I could only earn so much and go so far without getting some qualifications. So I made a start through college and eventually got to university."

It transpired that getting signed up to an Ordinary National Certificate was neither difficult nor hard to fund with support from employers and student grants. The ONC in turn fired an enthusiasm to read for an honours degree in civil engineering at Loughborough University followed by securing a decent job. The degree was achievable but finding a job was not so straightforward following the downturn in civil engineering after the UK trunk roads programme had been cut. Prospects suddenly appeared much less promising so Atack took a further bold step, to pursue a scholarship-funded master's degree in offshore structures at MIT (Massachusetts Institute of Technology). It was during this extended period of learning in the USA that an interest in offshore structures was developed, fuelled by a knowledge of the huge first generation North Sea projects such as BP's Forties oilfield project in the early 1970s.

Today, Atack brushes aside his MIT achievement as "a piece of personal development and a great experience" that allowed him to "get that first foot on the career ladder, feeling that I had already left it longer than I ought. I would have been 27 when I graduated from MIT".

Notwithstanding the late start, he knew he had accumulated some pretty good qualifications as currency, so he wrote to oil companies, interviewing with a bunch of them and securing several offers.

"I joined BP in 1977 as a production engineer, working offshore on Forties to begin with. BP seemed to fit my character at the time – a fun place to work, full of bright people shouldering particularly difficult challenges."

Going out to Forties marked a switch in Atack's career. He had studied offshore structures, possibly studied them to death.

"I went for an interview with BP for a structural engineering position, but when it came around to it, right at the head of the interview they said they weren't going to recruit that discipline and that they really wanted me to do something else.

Musical chairs – BP style

"I found out later that it was characteristic that BP was keen on having young, well-qualified people and it didn't particularly matter what discipline they came in with, there was a host of different roles they could be put to work in."

There are strong parallels between others in this book and Atack's experiences at this early stage in his oil career. Having been a late starter, he made up "lost" ground rapidly and found that his first job in the industry was different than originally envisaged. Also, like others, he already had practical albeit unrelated experience and had developed a measure of self-reliance.

"Obviously, at 27 I was a bit older than my peers but the engineering skill-set that I already had meant that I could turn my hand to various different areas. At the time, BP was very keen to build skills in the North Sea where a whole new industry was growing up.

"I was one of a large intake – I think over 100 graduates were taken in to BP and 40 of those came to Aberdeen.

"Working in BP was a bit of a privilege, indeed luxury. When you're in such a company with so many enthusiastic people, it's easy to get things done. Relationships tend to be quite easy because the work goes well."

In essence, Atack was nicely set up and, one supposes, could have made a life career out of BP. But he saw it differently by the mid-1990s when huge changes were under way at the company as it prepared to lead the North Sea outsourcing revolution.

"BP was going in a different direction to what I wanted to do and I wasn't best motivated by that, particularly as the skills that I had in production and development were no longer thought of as being core strengths that this oil major should develop, and that such duties should be performed by contractors in the future.

"The first move in that direction was the Foinaven oilfield development west of Shetland. Most of this project was contracted out. I had spent a lot of my career putting projects together and bringing them into production within BP; if this were to be done outside the company then my opportunities would also be outside BP."

He jumped in 1994, headed for local Aberdeen contractor Atlantic Power, which had been set up by Scots entrepreneur John Milligan, initially as a body shop. But the year before Atack joined, Atlantic Power set a North Sea milestone by becoming the only contractor to gain work on an offshore facility where day-to-day management was in its hands, with only the offshore installation managers (OIM) on the operating oil company's payroll. This was bold.

"Atlantic Power had just taken on the Gryphon job for Kerr-McGee and I think this was the first time in the [North Sea] industry a contractor had supplied most of the people and management thinking, on- and offshore, to develop and run an operation."

Atack joined because he knew Atlantic Power was bidding work with Oryx, which was due to take over management of the Hutton and Murchison fields from Conoco in 1995. This US corporation had decided that the best way forward was to contract out and keep its core management operation lean. It did not want to link with one of the larger contractors, which therefore worked in Atlantic Power's favour. He was to spend the next couple of years with Oryx, first doing the Hutton/Murchison transfer and then Ninian, by which time AP had developed a working formula and could do things a lot faster.

"Atlantic Power really looked like a good place for me to develop my ideas, where I would have the opportunity and leeway to do business the way I had been thinking about for a while.

"There were a lot of adjustments to be made, but probably not the ones you might imagine. The most straightforward part was actually getting the job done; I had run many jobs like this before in BP. The main adjustment was to become a contractor. Working for a large oil company, I had a lot of services available to me and that meant I could concentrate on the strategic side while others took care of detail.

"When you are a contractor and in charge of a project, you need to know how it's all going to work and, particularly, how you're going to get paid for it.

"I had a baptism certainly in understanding the very raw economics and commercial outcomes that might be expected and to deal with the client on a commercial as well as operational basis."

Cost-cutting opens opportunity door

It was also the time of CRINE (Cost Reduction Initiative for the New Era). Atack was already versed in the intent of this cross-UK offshore crusade largely driven by oil majors like BP and Shell. It was designed to strip cost out of the industry – that meant getting tough on the supply chain. He says that the switch from oil company to contractor made him reflect for a time on the knowledge that people in oil companies have about the impact they have on the people who perform their services and how ineffectual some of them can be in those relationships.

"I quickly realised there was a lot of value available to oil companies, which they had not been getting because of their conventional contractual relationships. My view of CRINE was that after some early successes it failed to deliver some of the bigger prizes.

"There was a continuous driving of costs out of the industry whereas, if oil company clients had stopped and asked the question about value, contractors would have been able to help them a lot in improving that value. To this day, a number of operators are still pushing the cost curve, in a relatively high oil price environment."

Atack had gone into Atlantic Power to manage the Oryx transfers and, at one point, this US independent was the primary client, accounting for a large proportion of turnover. But then a fresh client came on to the books in 1998; it was the Norwegian group PGS (Petroleum Geo-Services) with its Ramform Banff oil production vessel. In the event, PGS management decided that they liked the company so much that they couldn't do without owning it (shades of Victor Khayyam and his famous Remington shaver promotions).

Around the same time, Oryx, weakened by prevailing low oil prices, succumbed to a takeover by fellow US independent oil company Kerr-McGee. As both were by then Atlantic Power clients the Aberdeen company kept all the work, though one consequence was that KMG became the company's largest customer, by far.

Late 1998 saw PGS acquiring Atlantic Power to create PGS Production Services as part of a wider growth strategy for that company, and Atack quickly found himself tasked with sorting out the problems of the Conoco-operated Banff oilfield development, notably dealing with the radical ship which was to be used to produce and buffer-store output.

Starting in 1999, it took the best part of two years to get the ship working properly and achieving a 99% production uptime. Ultimately, this required alterations to the vessel at a Hamburg shipyard; since then there have been few significant problems.

"PGS was very disappointed with the initial performance of the vessel. There was a view that it was our inability to operate it that was the problem, rather than poor original design. We had to persuade the client [Conoco] that there would be an end to the problems on the vessel and we had to convince our own management [PGS] that we should take the cost and pain of removing the vessel for modifications.

"Looking back at it from 2005, I'm actually very pleased that I can say 'we fixed it'."

But what kept Atack at such a tough task?

"There was a job to do and I had started it. There wasn't an opportunity to walk away from the task of fixing the Ramform Banff. I won't leave a job half done when I've committed to do it."

As for any feeling of being made to carry the can, the response is: "The vessel had failed by the time I got to it. What was not enjoyable was carrying the can for the previous failure. But by fixing the problem the hope was that the failure would be purged."

And the wider PGS Production business at that time?

"I continued to participate in delivering the strategy that had been rolling since I joined and maybe a little before, namely this notion of operating other people's facilities as service operator (duty holder). This was the formative period for relationships with small oil companies that we thought would succeed in getting North Sea licences – companies such as Paladin and Venture."

Rescue at hand

Such relationship building was to transcend the sale of the business by PGS to Petrofac, whose engineering and construction business is rooted in Sharjah (UAE), but which is headquartered in London. The sale took place in December 2002. PGS was deeply in debt and in trouble. This in turn negatively impacted the Aberdeen business and threatened relationships with client oil companies.

"We [Aberdeen management] were very pleased when Petrofac came along. There was an element of *déjà vu* – the same enthusiasm for creating the 'service operator' concept in the UK and overseas."

By then, Atack was MD, having been rewarded two years earlier for sorting out Banff. But why him?

"Very simply because I was there and I was qualified," comes the response. "It hadn't been a job that I was pitching for. I was fully engaged in what I was doing and I would say that I didn't relish the potential of spending a lot more of my time in the public eye, pursuing our company's ambitions. It wasn't something I sought."

In terms of the 1,500-strong workforce it is probable that Atack's appointment to MD was widely acceptable as they already had ample experience of his quiet but authoritative style while in charge of operations.

"The previous management structure had me looking after the operations, while others handled business development and strategy. So there wasn't much change in terms of leadership from the people perspective; it was simply a case of my stepping up to take more responsibility. Other people followed in to manage the growing operations."

The public thing was perhaps the least desirable aspect of the job, but Atack wisely took on the responsibility and with verve having realised that, if he were to take the job as MD, it was necessary to develop a high profile for the business or there wouldn't be any point in doing the job.

"What we were trying to do was to pursue a particular solution in the industry and that meant we had to create a market for it. This meant we had to persuade people that this was the logical thing to do. So we were not simply carrying on in the same way, we were creating a new business.

"That meant we had to share our opinion about Petrofac's 'service operator' model, and hopefully people would sit up and take notice. That was the only way we were going to grow our business, by having a view, having an opinion, sharing it, being controversial at times, but not being part of the background.

"I decided there were a number of issues, campaigns, things that I was passionate about that I was quite happy to talk about, and that I truly owned those subjects. It has become easier over the past few years to define what those things are and to go out and talk about them and I guess it becomes self-fulfilling.

"However, I'm very clear that, when I'm asked to join in with an industry initiative, I won't do it unless I can spend enough time to contribute effectively. If it's not my subject, not something that I really care about, I won't do it.

"Subjects that I typically pick up are also subjects that are close to the area of business that we're trying to pursue. One of my topics just now is to ensure that non-industry people understand that there is quite a lot more life left in the North Sea. This needs to be a campaign that lots of people get on with or the industry will keep on talking it down, people will believe us and indeed it won't have a future. This is something I'll take every opportunity to push."

But how does Atack lead a business that today accounts for some 2,500 North Sea personnel plus a further 500 elsewhere? There are tremendous leadership issues and he has the incredible challenge of encouraging young people into the business, let alone the industry as a whole.

Be a team player

The reply: "If you took it on as a single individual's responsibility, it would be quite horrible and very daunting. But you cannot be successful on your own, without quite a lot of support, and that's not simply people doing what you ask them to do; it's people having original thought and taking on projects of their own. That way it's neither horrible nor daunting.

"I'm not sure that I intend for people to buy-in to me as an independent leader; I hope I have a shared vision with enough people so that most of us say: 'These are the things we're trying to do.' There's a clear understanding, it makes sense, and people are then motivated to follow that lead. It's not a single leader issue for me.

"I'm here today, but there'll be someone else here tomorrow. It's part of my duty to make sure that there are lots of other capable people who can take on my role, encourage the company to grow, who can engage with clients, management and politicians."

To young people – students – the Atack message is simple: "I'm not very keen on the rote subject of management.

"For any individual embarking on a career, what I would say is, try to take a stand about something every day. Hopefully, after a while, those opinions will become real for you and start to converge until you begin to define yourself and what you want out of life, and what it is that you get passionate about. It's only if you have an opinion about things that you will be noticed in the business world and nobody's going to promote you unless you have a view.

"You'll find the downside in the Beatles song, *Nowhere Man* – 'doesn't have a point of view, knows not where he's going to ...'

"If you do have a point of view, then you will likely know where you're going, and will have a very good chance of getting there."

2 NEIL BRUCE

GLOBAL MOGUL

NEIL BRUCE

Name	Neil Bruce
Company	AMEC
Company turnover	AMEC group turnover is £5 billion
Current position	Managing Director, AMEC oil and gas
Place of Birth	Brought up in Portlethen
Education	Portlethen Primary, Mackie Academy, Chartered marine engineer, MBA
First job	Variety of development roles with Brown & Root initially on the Brent C hook-up project
Best business decision	Early on in my career I learnt that it was essential for the business to hire or progress people better than me
Worst business decision	Thinking it was possible to consolidate for a while; competition in our industry will quickly erode your advantage
Which company in the upstream oil and gas industry do you admire and why?	Apart from AMEC ... ? Schlumberger is a truly professional organisation and a great example of a global company that deserves recognition ... investing both in people and technology
Biggest dislike of the industry	The various industry initiatives that don't appear to go anywhere or add any value
Advice to anyone considering a career in the oil industry	The future you imagine is possible within the oil and gas industry, but you must take a proactive approach, and accept equal responsibility in creating it, don't just rely on a company handing it to you
What do you think of management gurus?	I don't believe in generalising, I've met very inspirational "gurus" through to very poor consultants – and I have learnt from both
Favourite pastime	I enjoy watching live sport, particularly Aberdeen Football Club and Formula 1. Thankfully I also enjoy travel – which is an essential part of my job
Favourite book	I found *Good to Great* (Jim Collins) a genuinely inspiring read
Who or what is your inspiration?	Alex Ferguson, a great example of someone who delivered demanding performance and relentless improvement
Any further ambitions?	Absolutely, for me this is just the beginning, I thrive on team collective success/sense of achievement
Favourite quote/saying	The more I practice, the luckier I get (attributed to Jack Nicklaus)

NEIL BRUCE

GLOBAL MOGUL

In December 2004, AMEC Oil & Gas carried off the Scottish Council Development & Industry's President's Award for outstanding global achievement and there to receive the accolade was its beaming MD, Neil Bruce.

Some 23 years on since he secured his first job in the energy business, and that was the only one that he had ever applied for, Bruce was in the mood to celebrate; but he was even more excited a few months later when AMEC finally acquired Paragon Engineering, a top US oilfield engineering house based in Houston. It was the culmination (for a while at least) of a six-year drive by the UK group to build a meaningful presence in North America. Not only that, the group had got to the position where it could implement its six-hub global energy model – essentially a transnational business focused on oil and gas and where the respective centres are to all intents and purposes on an equal footing, with each reporting to Bruce in Aberdeen.

Being in the driving seat of a business worth around $2.3 billion in 2004 is far removed from the Aberdeen lad who had no fixed idea on a career; rather, his ambition was to play for the local football team until the realisation dawned in his mid-teens that he wasn't good enough.

Having said he had no particular career aspiration, what Bruce did develop at a very early stage was an interest in business.

"I did economics and accountancy at school but, socially, it was music and football big-time. I certainly wasn't tucked away reading books."

He eschewed the idea of university, preferring Dundee College and a Higher National Certificate in business studies. The immediate aim was to get working.

"A lot of my friends went to university straight away but I didn't fancy the four-year slog. I wanted to get stuck into working. Stigma? No way. I wanted a job – money coming in, being able to pursue my interests. Later I did go back to the academic thing, as it became something I wanted to pursue and I suppose I did it all rather back to front."

Oil had started to influence the northeast Scottish economy and it seemed the obvious choice, with good money as the bait, so Bruce applied for a job at offshore contracting company Brown & Root, which was working on completing a big new Shell oil production platform, known as Brent Charlie, at the time.

"I spoke to the careers people at Brown & Root and joined the company on a scheme similar to a graduate scheme whereby they gave me a great background in training.

"I did four years, with the bulk of training in the first two. I was on a managed career path where they gave me experience in various departments, and I was offshore within two weeks of joining.

"It was junior management stuff in various departments – construction, commercial, planning and scheduling, project control – plus I was often offshore. It was a really good background."

Bruce had landed on his feet aged 20 – straight out of college and into the glamour business of the day. It also became the only job he ever applied for. An initial spell in the North Sea was followed by assignment to Bahrain and then back to the UK, always in management roles of one form or another and generally focused on the project control business side, field engineering, and site construction management. The last four years of Bruce's 1979-89 sojourn with B&R was focused on being project manager of new field developments. That decade spanned both the most dynamic and the most difficult years of the North Sea industry – the tremendous build-up of the early 1980s, which ended almost overnight with the oil price crash of 1986, followed by uncertain recovery.

Unquestionably, Bruce received an excellent grounding and above all recognised the value of teamwork and the buzz it could impart.

"I like the discipline of set goals and targets that are measurable and you can see whether the team is performing well and achieving what they're supposed to."

Cutting leadership teeth

"The first time I really led was when we were working on part of the Morecambe Bay gasfield complex hook-up. I led a punch-out/completions team to a couple of the fabrication yards at the time. That was the first time I had really been responsible for going outside the office with a bunch of people working under me. I was about 25 at the time.

"The fantastic thing about the oil and gas industry in those days, and more so than now, was the fact that the opportunities available were almost limitless. No-one stood in your way though, ultimately, you had to have the ability."

As for the management style that prevailed in the 1970s and 1980s, it was a case of get out there and get on with it.

"But I don't think B&R ever let you go away and do things that you were clearly not capable of doing. They certainly gave you the opportunity to prove yourself and if you didn't deliver the results, I guess you were pulled back and redirected. But I never experienced that. It just seemed to be, here's the next bit – I can do that – then on to the next bit and so on. The market had yet to mature and lots of things were being learned by everyone.

"Maybe I have rose-tinted glasses about it all. But it seemed like it was about getting things done in those days."

This was a period of big projects, big budgets and large supply chain margins. Not that cost and scheduling didn't matter, because they did, but Bruce cannot recall agonising over budgets and plans for months on end as tends to be the case today. Management was simpler.

Given his close involvement with big oilfield infrastructure projects, Bruce was arguably more vulnerable to the 1986 global oil price crash than most of the other moguls featured in this book.

"I was on a Southern North Sea gasfield development for Conoco at the time. While there was indeed a downturn, I was living in London and the crisis did not assume the stark reality that it did in centres like Aberdeen."

How did B&R build Neil Bruce the manager? At that time the company had a policy of investing in its people; training was on the job, plus there was a general management training course that culminated in a formal examination. This training was to have a lasting impression.

"The thing that stuck with me is, wherever I've been since, I'm very keen that we give people the opportunity to develop themselves. It's not just about having a good graduate scheme; I think it's really important that people are given the maximum chance of career development so they can go out and grab opportunities. Those who generally succeed are the ones who go for it.

"Today at AMEC, I spend time with our graduates, including hosting lunches that are designed to get to know them. The one question that usually comes up is: 'What can I do to give myself the best chance to succeed?' The answer is usually exactly the same, which is: 'Don't sit there, do the course and then wait for people to feed you something; go out and create your own career."

Back to Brown & Root. Ten years in, Bruce decided that it was time for a change. Had he stayed, he felt that the next few years would be more or less a repeat of the prior decade. It was time for a new experience, so Bruce rapidly decided to become a consultant.

"Wisely or stupidly I set up a consultancy in London that would focus on project management services. I did various pieces of work for different oil companies. I was a consultant for eight years in total."

Bruce was a one-man band, enjoying his independence and having the freedom to select his own pace and client base. Basically it was work, work, work. The notion of taking a block of time off to go away and pursue something else was not on the agenda.

Back to school

Yet, in the middle of all of this, he decided the time was ripe to go back to school and pursued marine architecture at the University of Newcastle upon Tyne, while still keeping the consultancy going. The objective was to become a chartered engineer, something he had ample experience in. The whole process, including dissertation, was made easier because Bruce was able to draw on his experience as an oil and gas industry professional.

During the final period as a consultant when he was working primarily with the oil company Atlantic Richfield (Arco), Bruce came under pressure to consider joining the company and, in 1996, the decision was made to sign on shortly after completing what he describes as a tough and demanding project.

"This was the Trent/Tyne gasfields development in the southern North Sea. There had been huge challenges on that one and it turned into a bit of a slog at the end. But a couple of people I knew at AMEC had been talking with me for about a year on and off asking me if I fancied a change and I had always said I wasn't really interested.

"But, having got to the end of Trent/Tyne, I started to think about what was next. And what was next was another Trent/Tyne or smaller. It then struck me that I had got back into the recycle thing, so it was time for a change. That was when I started serious discussions with AMEC with the result that I joined the company's Hadrian fabrication yard complex, Wallsend upon Tyne at the start of 1997."

In essence, Bruce's career path had run: contractor, consultant, oil company and back to contractor, but this time as a director. The period 1995 through 1997 was a relatively prosperous time for the North Sea, with a number of significant projects such as Scott, Andrew and Harding taken forward against a background of heavy cost-cutting. There were two objectives to the Bruce appointment at AMEC – boosting safety performance and profitability, the latter being highly pertinent given the oil companies' obsession with slashing capital budgets.

"The job seemed oddly simple and that was one of the appealing things about it. I didn't have a job description and heaps of objectives. I was given the latitude to go in, figure it out and get on with the task.

"A big drive had started to boost North Sea safety performance about that time and that included the fabrication sector. For me personally, safety had always been very important.

"When you're in the supply chain as a contractor you have one view on it; when you're an operator you have another view; and then, when you're back in the supply chain with the likes of AMEC, and on the fabrication side moreover, the perspective is different again.

"The real common thread throughout is that it's about people and it's personal.

"For me, until you get to the point where it's people and personal then I don't think you can get to the areas that are important, and how you can bring about improvement, otherwise it is too high-level, remote and systems, as opposed to people and behaviours."

Bruce spent two years in this new role. But did he succeed?

"I think we did. We completed and delivered on new projects, we met all our objectives and, from a safety perspective, during that period, we improved sevenfold on the statistics. On the two objectives – deliver customer satisfaction allied to profitable work and improved safety – I think I succeeded."

Magic of buy-in

A personal satisfaction for Bruce is that the best safety performance achieved at Wallsend was actually after he left the yard to take up another role at AMEC. "Maybe the guys that followed were even better," he adds.

But how did he get buy-in from the Wallsend workforce in the first place? Bruce says the formula was simple. He took a personal interest and tried to get out on-site every day, unless he was away. It was about getting the hard hat on and going around the yard having chats.

"To begin with I was viewed fairly sceptically, but I think that, after showing face day after day, week after week, month after month, a genuine interest started to develop.

"I worked on revamping our safety procedures, inductions; we introduced an interactive induction system rather than leaving it up to the guys to look at or ignore a video. That applied to everyone and not just the yard's shop floor. I hope that the guys at all levels started to accept that safety was for everybody and not just the workforce. I did get a sense that not everyone saw it that way at first."

What is the Bruce management style and what defines it?

"Getting the right team around you, for a start – and that's about applying experience and gut instinct. One thing I firmly believe in is having a team of mixed capabilities and strengths and getting them to spark off against one another. And, while some people are ideas generators or initiators, others are perhaps better at taking a task and seeing it through.

"I do like to map out and have clear, measurable targets. And that takes various forms. If you're on a project, it would tend to be around health, safety and environment (HSE), planning scheduling, costing, budgets and the likes. If you're on a different kind of contract, such as operations and maintenance, then it would be around the effectiveness of the maintenance regime you have in place; if you're running a business, for us it's around four basic parameters – safety, financial performance, customer satisfaction and people.

"It doesn't take a lot of time and effort to come up with a view on what success could look like – on an annual basis, end of a defined period, end of contract – and if you can define what success would look like then you can define what key performance indicators or measures need to be in place in order to see whether you're on track. And then, once you've laid that out, it's important to get the right people into the right slots in order to go forward."

It was during his time at Wallsend that Bruce decided to pursue an MBA, so he returned to Newcastle University on a part-time basis. While he insists this was of his own volition, there was also subtle pressure from the top for him to build his credentials as he was being groomed for higher things.

"In discussions around succession planning and how you actually move through the company, the MBA was seen as something that certainly would do no harm."

He happens to feel strongly about continuous learning. "I think the whole thing to do with continuous learning has become more important to me personally as time has moved on. It doesn't have to be anything formal at university. It can be travel, different cultures, something new. I have this desire for something new."

Back to Aberdeen

Back to the Bruce career path: in 1999 the decision was made to shift him out of Tyneside and send him to Aberdeen, which was suffering at the hands of the late 1997 through 1999 oil price slump. His new brief covered all business out of Aberdeen, plus Wallsend, the Yarmouth facility and engineering in London.

"When I returned to Aberdeen (for the first time in his working career), that was when, through various internal strategy sessions, we embarked on an examination of the long-term future of the North Sea and the implications for AMEC. That was when we decided to internationalise the business. Indeed I was asked to do it. At that time, apart from a bit of work in Norway, we were essentially North Sea."

The next steps can only be described as bold, at least in the context of oil and gas. AMEC had long had an international spread, especially in east/

southeast Asia, which also turned out to be the starting point for the Bruce-driven internationalisation drive. This is where the first major project – Malampaya – was secured. It was followed by a pioneering arrangement with the Koreans. Elsewhere, the company has successfully penetrated Russia and, most recently, consolidated its North America position (see above).

Today, as head of oil and gas (up and downstream), Bruce arguably holds the prize brief of the corporation. When offered the job, this modest, rather understated individual says he simply grabbed it.

"I replied within a couple of seconds. It never entered my head to sit and think about it. It's just a bigger version of running a team."

The current role is far removed from being a one-man band consultant; leading a business employing more than 3,000 individuals poses many challenges, not least sustaining effective communications.

"I think a lot of what you do is the same each time. It's about being clear what the objectives are, being clear about what you and the company stand for and it's about getting the right and appropriate team with the right mix around you in order to deliver against that.

"I would say that clarity of purpose and delivery is important, I like to operate within a team. I think it's really important that team members have their views and pull from their strengths but, ultimately, it's also important that, since I'm leading the team, I'm clear about the decisions I make and the direction I take. After that, I expect everyone in that team to actually get behind.

"I played a huge amount of sport so I have a lot of experience of what is possible with a bunch of individuals. Indeed this is more easily shown through sport than in a company. It is much clearer. I remember that, when on the pitch we were at our personal best when working together as a team. We achieved more that way. There's power in the team.

"Also, there's limited short-term success in treating people in a manner where you're either bullying or shouting or somehow being the star performer in all of this. It's not on.

"As management, our main role should be to provide all the people who work for us in various forms the best opportunity for them to be successful and then, ultimately, we'll be successful. It's about doing the right thing for your people and the business.

"Right now I feel as if I'm in the middle of something that's exciting, progressing – there's something about creating an international business – a British business too – and its energy."

3 DREELAN BROTHERS

FILIAL MOGULS

THE DREELAN BROTHERS
LEFT TO RIGHT: CIARAN, SEAN, TOMMY, MIKE

FACT FILE

Name	Ciaran Dreelan
Company	Qserv Ltd
Company turnover	£17 m
Current position	Well Services Director
Place of birth	Co. Wexford, Ireland.
Education	Secondary school level, HNC Mechanical Engineering
First job	Service Operator in Well Services
Best business decision	Starting Qserv
Worst business decision	Thankfully not aware of it yet
Which company in the upstream oil and gas industry do you admire and why?	Qserv, because of the admiration for the staff within the company
Biggest dislike of the industry	Bureaucracy, too many reasons why not to do something
Advice to anyone considering a career in the oil industry	I have found it to be a good industry and rewarding; however, you must be prepared to put in the effort
What do you think of management gurus?	Not a lot, if you want to do something go ahead and do it. You do not need a guru to tell you what you already know
Favourite pastime	Cycling and spending time with my kids
Favourite book	Don't have one, but read an excellent book recently about the oil industry in the North Sea over the past 40 years
Who or what is your inspiration?	Inspiration is to be successful and grow Qserv to be the top service provider in our field
Any further ambitions?	Continue what we have started with Qserv and spend more time with my kids
Favourite quote/saying	It can be done and will be done

FACTFILE

Name	Sean Dreelan
Company	Qserv Ltd
Company turnover	£17 m
Current position	Director
Place of Birth	Co. Wexford, Ireland
Education	Secondary school level
First Job	Carpenter
Best business decision	To own my own company
Worst business decision	Thankfully, none
Which company in the upstream oil and gas industry do you admire and why?	Qserv, due to the people we have working for us, and our equipment
Biggest dislike of the industry	Very long hours due to client demand in the industry
Advice to anyone considering a career in the oil industry	Never claim you know it all and always ask questions
What do you think of management gurus?	They're not willing to listen to all sides of the story
Favourite pastime	Family fun and holidays with the kids
Favourite book	No favourite book but read a lot of technical literature
Who or what is your inspiration?	Family
Any further ambitions?	Continue to build Qserv as a profitable company
Favourite quote/saying	You will never know it all

FACT FILE

Name	Tommy Dreelan
Company	Qserv Ltd
Company turnover	£17 m
Current position	Managing Director
Place of birth	Co. Wexford, Ireland
Education	Secondary school level and Mechanical Engineering HNC at night school in Dublin over a 3-year period
First job	Fitter plumber
Best business decision	To start my own business
Worst business decision	None. However, some could have been better if more detailed planning had been done
Which company in the upstream oil and gas industry do you admire and why?	WoodGroup and KCA Deutag as they are ambitious and well managed, plus many of our clients' companies
Biggest dislike of the industry	Low return – high capital investment in our service lines
Advice to anyone considering a career in the oil industry?	Never be afraid to ask and learn all you can; if you want to be successful, work hard and you will achieve your goals
What do you think of management gurus?	They are not experts but think they know it all
Favourite pastime	Family and cars, especially steam cars
Favourite book	Don't have a favourite but one that stands out is *How to Win Friends and Influence People* by Dale Carnegie.
Who or what is your inspiration?	To exceed our clients' expectations
Any further ambitions?	Further develop and build Qserv as a profitable business to meet/exceed our clients' demands
Favourite quote/saying	Let's have the results and not the excuses

Name	Michael Dreelan
Company	Qserv Ltd
Company turnover	£17 m
Current position	Engineering Director
Place of birth	Co. Wexford, Ireland
Education	Secondary school level and Mechanical Engineering
First job	Mechanical fitter
Best business decision	To start my own business
Worst business decision	Thankfully no disasters to date, but not complacent
Which company in the upstream oil and gas industry do you admire and why?	All private companies who venture into this sector, because it is a competitive and difficult market
Biggest dislike of the industry	Bureaucracy – not enough of a "can do" attitude
Advice to anyone considering a career in the oil industry	Aim to be the best in whatever sector you choose. Work hard and you can be rewarded and, like anything in life, you only get out what you are prepared to put in
What do you think of management gurus?	If you need to consult one, I think you have a bigger problem in the company than you know about
Favourite pastime	Spending time with family and working on steam engines and vintage vehicles
Favourite book	Don't have one, I have never read a book from cover to cover
Who or what is your inspiration?	Isambard Kingdom Brunel
Any further ambitions?	To continue growing Qserv to be a successful and "best in its class" company
Favourite quote/saying	Never say never

FACT FILE

DREELAN BROTHERS

FILIAL MOGULS

In traditional family firms, having several siblings working alongside one another is still fairly commonplace, usually with the oldest male assuming the most senior role. The same broad rule applies in farming, except that, while young offspring rapidly get used to the idea of working at an early age and co-operating out of necessity, once they reach adulthood the farm will generally pass to the oldest male.

In the UK oil and gas industry, while there are examples of, say, two brothers or a brother and sister teaming up in an SME, there may be just one firm where four brothers are working alongside one another to a common purpose – Qserv of Portlethen, by Aberdeen.

The Dreelan brothers – Tommy, Mike, Sean and Ciaran – are of Irish (Wexford) farming stock. Seventeen years separate the oldest, Tommy (late 40s), from the youngest, Ciaran (early 30s). They say no favouritism has been shown over the years and that they are in business together on the basis of merit. Judging by the career paths of three – each worked for the energy services giant, Schlumberger – this is true. People only get to work for Schlumberger because they have directly demonstrated their capability or potential. Filial recommendations count for nothing.

The first of eight Dreelan siblings, Tommy was also first out of the nest, so to speak. He left school aged 16 to join a heating and ventilation company as an apprentice.

"As soon as I left I regretted it and within three months I started going to night school. The engineering company I worked for was based in Dublin and I went to Bolton Street College of Technology. I did three years of night school in mechanical engineering, but didn't take the exams, the reason being that I was transferred from Dublin to Mullingar in the centre of Ireland."

While the job was decent enough, he was looking for something better. Ireland 30 years ago was not the booming economy that it is today.

"I had a friend who graduated from Trinity College, Dublin as a geologist and had started working in geo-services overseas. When on leave at home, he would tell me about the oil industry and that's what got my interest.

"It was just by coincidence that Schlumberger had an advertisement in the *Irish Independent*. It was looking for engineers to train up for the overseas market. I applied and got a job. I was put through the Dowell Schlumberger training school in France, went from there to Libya, from Libya to the Middle East, Middle East to London and, in 1981, I ended up in Aberdeen. All this happened over a period of six and a half years.

"Getting that first job was a great opportunity. I worked my way up through the business, from field engineer to looking after the technical section and sales out of Aberdeen. There, my task was primarily looking after clients, business development and technical sales.

"With Schlumberger, I thought I would have been there forever because that was the message that was portrayed to everyone that worked for them, that you had a job for life, and it is. Then they decided that I was to be transferred to Norway at the end of 1985, but I chose to resign and do my own thing – set up my own business."

Supply chain blue chip, good money, good future, money in the bank but not yet a family. Life was good for this Irish batchelor. But he wanted independence.

"It had been simmering at the back of the mind for two years but I never thought I could do it. I received loads of encouragement because my position in business development and sales meant that I was spending a lot of time in the marketplace with clients."

Client feedback was that there was a need for local competition to the multinational service big names – BJ, Halliburton and Schlumberger. So he resigned and established Progenitive Services Limited (PSL).

"In some ways I couldn't have set it up at a worse time because of the 1986 oil price crash. However, there were also a lot of opportunities. Oil companies were cutting back on costs."

Independence road

"The crash opened the door for a new independent well services company to come in and be really focused on what the client was looking for and to do it at a competitive rate yet also build a business. But some of those who had encouraged me to get out of Schlumberger were not forthcoming with contracts, at least not initially. When it came to the crunch, they were not so sure."

What got PSL moving was the decision to trade in equipment and oilfield chemicals – with the occasional bit of well services work. Initially it was just Tommy Dreelan, a secretary and someone with a mechanical aptitude to work on equipment. The initial emphasis was to design and build equipment, notably oilfield pumping units and tanks.

Curiously, it was Occidental that gave the fledgling business its first break. This same company did a similar thing for another subject of this book, Larry Kinch, who also worked for Schlumberger. While he did indeed deliver, Dreelan also admits that he cut things a bit fine at times when PSL was in its infancy. An example of sailing close to the wind was talking to two or three clients at the same time and promising them all the same thing when that was patently impossible because of insufficient resources. But somehow it all worked out.

PSL was at Westhill for 18 months, then moved to a site near Aberdeen Harbour, then in 1990 moved to Portlethen where its headquarters were purpose built.

Tommy Dreelan has made a profit from almost day one and certainly the first year of trading. Indeed, the first 10 years of PSL saw a compound growth rate of 46% per annum. But how was this achieved without outgrowing the company's resource or even being in the dangerous position of over-trading?

"By being surrounded by the right people. In those early days, profit margins were higher than now. Every penny we made was reinvested in the business. I was married by then and had started a family, but we honestly took very little out of the business. Until the day that we sold PSL, we only took enough to live on."

That said, it is possible to misjudge, as he acknowledges.

"There are people who come out of large companies and go into small ones, but then fail to adapt, not because they're bad people – they could be excellent – but the resources they previously had at their fingertips are no longer available, they have to get involved themselves. It is fair to say that some of these individuals do not work out.

"I've always believed that working in a small company is more difficult than in a big one as it's harder to adapt. You have to be very flexible to turn your hand to doing different things, whatever the requirements of the time. That said, you also have to be careful that you don't have individuals getting involved in something for which they clearly don't have the capability.

"But there are a lot of people who, if they have the willpower and really want to do it, they'll learn anyway. Training and tuition can make the difference. Indeed training is absolutely critical and remains so for us.

"But some people think that training is going away for a week on a course somewhere. However, all that may be needed in some cases is half an hour or training on a specific topic. It could be just a toolbox talk – five minutes. We do a lot of toolbox talks, they're absolutely essential."

By 1990, when PSL made the switch from Westhill to Portlethen, the head-count was about 100 and turnover some £9 million. This compares with a first-year turnover of £560,000 and a handful or so members of staff.

Four Dreelan drive

Also, by then, Tommy had gathered his three brothers into the business. But why and how was it achieved given that filial rivalries can tear many a family apart?

"We are pretty close though we do lead our own lives; we're not in each other's pockets though we share some hobbies.

"When you're brought up with the kind of background we have, you have to work from a very young age, or at least that's how it was in those days. You had to do it – any spare time you had. There was always a lot to do and it got all of us working close together.

"What's interesting is that Mike, Sean and I all worked for Schlumberger, we all left school early and we all served our time – Sean as a carpenter while Mike and I served at the same heating and ventilation company. But when we worked for Schlumberger, none of us were in the same area together. Mike went to Libya, for example."

It is fair to say that Mike and Sean became involved because of their older brother, but only insofar as he alerted them about available jobs. The youngest, Ciaran, came to Aberdeen to work during holidays. After leaving school he eventually decided to study for a Higher National Diploma in engineering.

As for any prior thought of their joining PSL, Tommy says he set the firm up without reference to any of his brothers. He just got on with it.

Mike was first to get involved and that was while on a rotation out of Libya. He came visiting when Tommy was building his first pump unit. The two had a common interest in doing this and Mike was asked if he was willing to give it a go, especially as his elder brother needed someone with an equipment design and build track record.

Sean joined at more or less the same time because there was the need for experienced field personnel and he possessed what was needed.

Ciaran was last to join PSL and then as an employee with no boardroom rights. He had to wait until 2003 when the brothers set up a new venture called Qserv, following the sale of PSL.

Family is family, business is business, so how do the Dreelans strike a balance that works and avoids filial jealousies, which it clearly does?

For example, why has Tommy traditionally led the way and always been the spokesman, even for this book? Is it simply because he's the oldest and most experienced and, after all, it was his initiative that established PSL in the first place?

"There never has been conflict," insists Tommy. "It's fair to say that there can be differences of opinion as with any work colleague. But that doesn't mean that we don't get on or argue.

"Everyone has their ideas, maybe about doing something differently, but we deal with it just like working with any other colleague. Despite saying, well, it just so happens that the four shareholders of this business (Qserv) happen to be brothers, it is not run as a family business. That is a conscious decision."

Regarding Ciaran and PSL with three in the boardroom and one not, this was not an issue either, as far as Tommy is concerned.

"Turn it around the other way, why would we favour Ciaran being in the boardroom over any other employee just because he's family?

"That said, we've avoided the pitfall of filling the Qserv boardroom with brothers. We don't run it as a family business because to attract the right people to work for us, the right calibre of management, it is very important that we are all seen as individuals. We just happen to be brothers, we just happen to be shareholders. We want everyone to be open and honest and avoid the brothers ganging together thing where people feel excluded.

"This is very, very important because we want to grow the business, and that means having the right people in the right places. If we had a closely knit family-run business, that would put such people off and damage the business.

"When we have a board meeting, it involves only the people you really need to have there, and it's important to ensure that outcomes are disseminated as appropriate. We do our best to get it right over communications."

But how is this accomplished with a business as sophisticated as Qserv or the prior business PSL, as none of the brothers has any formal management schooling, except the occasional short course, and yet they assiduously train their workforce?

"I think it has just happened," says Tommy. "Our learning has been on the job – constantly."

PSL goldmine

Flipping back to PSL and its development, that came to an end with an ultimately successful offer by NatWest Equity Partners. NatWest made its first move in 1997, but it took nine months for the organisation to get a meeting with the Dreelans.

"How they approached it was to write a couple of letters to me. They got no response," says Tommy. "I had never heard of them, I really didn't read the letters and I honestly thought this was a bank wanting to see if they could develop a relationship with us in order to lend money. It's the usual story, when you want something, no one wants to talk to you; when you don't want them, everyone is at your doorstep.

"For a few years leading up to that, competitors talked to us. But we never developed any of those discussions. We kept on saying that PSL was not for sale. Nine months on they went through an intermediary, Ken Murray. One of the NatWest guys, Dave Sneddon, was at that time involved with the local enterprise company Scottish Enterprise Grampian. He knew of us and that's how it all started.

"Ken came to us and said he knew the business was not for sale but sold the idea of a chat at least. I had lunch with him. It was suggested that, even though the business was not for sale, what harm would there be in having a meeting with NatWest. So a meeting was arranged.

"They came so well prepared that they had an offer on the table at the first meeting, which lasted 45 minutes. Mike and I attended. We said; 'Guys, we're not for sale.' They said: 'Maybe you should consider it.'

"So we asked about the terms and the reply was: 'We want you guys to stay and run the business.'

"I said: 'Hang on, why are we having this discussion? If we're going to sell the business, why would we be staying with it? It would have enough value in it now that, hopefully, we wouldn't have to work again. It would be different if it was only £1 million and we still had to work.'

"They asked us how we saw the situation. Our reply was that there was a good management team in place; we hadn't developed it that way because we had been so focused on building PSL on a day-to-day basis. We never had an exit plan.

"Two weeks later they came back with a detailed offer, saying they would have to be satisfied that the management team was capable of running the company.

"They said: 'Here's the offer, it's a cash deal.'

"It took two months to complete. We sold PSL for £45.5 million."

Ciaran remained on the payroll while his director brothers exited stage left.

Tommy adds: "It took two weeks for it to really sink in as to what we had done and then we asked whether we had done the right thing.

"Also, what is interesting, and I've seen it so many times in companies where people take their eye off the ball, right up to the last minute of the PSL deal, we did not get involved any more than was absolutely necessary.

"Until the day it happened, if it hadn't happened, it wouldn't have bothered us. It was business as usual. Maybe in our minds we thought the sale would never happen, or, because we had no goals for it to happen, we always felt we would have died with the company.

"A lot of it was because we had grown the business; there was loyalty towards our people. It was an emotional time. But if you had told me ahead of the deal that it would be emotional, I would never have believed you. It was."

Playing is boring

Out of the door, stack of money in the bank, chance of a sabbatical. But that didn't last long. Playing got boring.

"We're the type of guys who like to be busy all the time. The way we were raised, from the time we could walk we were on our feet working – even driving tractors at an extremely young age. Because of that it's in our system and always will be."

In essence, selling PSL left three of the brothers marooned. They could talk the business but weren't doing it and that engendered frustration.

"To be honest, we were missing it – not the tensions, but the buzz," says Tommy. "Encouragement from the marketplace, plus we were getting itchy feet, led us to launching our next business, Carrack. We could have set up in business the next day competing against PSL outwith the North Sea, but we didn't.

Carrack, an oilfield equipment trading house, was about keeping all the connections warm. It was then and remains a useful business venture in its own right. But there were no thoughts as such of going back into a similar line of business to PSL.

"We really didn't think we would go back into the business again, not for any positive or negative reasons. We knew we would need to do something and Carrack gave us that; also spare time to do things with our steam engines and cars. We hadn't had the time in the past to do that; now was the time to make up for lost ground in that regard."

Nevertheless, towards the end of 2001, the decision was taken to set up another business that resembled the PSL concept and it was established in November that year after barely two or three months of in-depth thinking and planning.

The Dreelans had the luxury of having money in the bank to launch Qserv fully funded from their own resources. That said, they do plan to "take borrowings in" as the company grows. It's about spreading risk.

"When I originally set up PSL, no one was interested in talking to me," recalls Tommy. "It was just a relationship with my own bank manager at the time that enabled me to get a loan. He liked the story.

Another sharp difference is that, with Qserv, the brothers know exactly where they are going. That was not the case with PSL.

"We never had a business plan, right to the end. However, what became important in the final four or five years at PSL was an annual plan putting budgets in place. From my own point of view, I came from a background where I had no experience in financial planning; the banks never put any pressure on us for financial planning as we grew because the company was generating cash and lots of it.

"The approach has been different with Qserv because we've learned a lot from the past. We've learned that you do need a plan in place. If I'm being honest we don't put a huge amount of time into it. We do have budgets and we have guys running the various departments and they need to be responsible and accountable; we need better planning because this business is growing a lot faster than we grew PSL. First year turnover was around £3 million (2001), £7.5 million (2002) and £12.5 million in 2004. This year the forecast is £17 million."

The Dreelans are in essence repeating the successes of PSL, but with a lot more experience at their backs than before. They should be able to avoid mistakes, though Tommy insists there were no disasters in the past. He points out that creating a new oil service business today is a lot different from building it in the past. It's a completely different market. In the past, the market was such that you could go to a client, get a commitment from that client about a job and then you would look at how you were going to source the equipment and people.

"You cannot do that today. If you can't demonstrate to the client that you have the resources – people, equipment and facilities, all of the HSEQ (health, safety, environment and quality assurance) systems – you'll not work for them. That's one thing we got right at Qserv from the day we started this business."

Filial pecking order

So what about the filial pecking order and boardroom attitudes? It's rather simple, really.

"Some of it is habit. The key point is that we discussed this when setting up Qserv – who is the right person to do what," says Tommy. When we looked back we agreed it had all worked well in the past, so why change it.

"If you ask who could do who's job, Ciaran could do my job no problem. In fact he would probably do it better than me as he has a different skill-set and more education than I have. He's still only 30. Could Mike or Sean do the MD's job? I would say no. If you asked could I do Mike's job, no I couldn't do it; nor Sean's.

"But we're part of a wider management team. We understand the strengths and weaknesses of the rest of the management team and they understand ours as well. That's what makes us really work.

"Yes, MD is my title, but I'm not the only one who makes the decisions. Many are made by the others, particularly Ciaran's group. People get on with making their own decisions. They may run things past me as a balancing board.

"We challenge one another all of the time. I'm not saying we don't make mistakes because we do. As for tensions in-company, we don't take the rows home.

"If we see any of our people having disagreements with one another – these happen – we say 'Guys, do not leave here until you get that sorted.' I hate going home with something on my mind perhaps because I had an argument and didn't sort it out."

The last words go to Ciaran as, should Tommy drop out, the mutual view among the brothers is that he is MD material.

"This is the second time around [on the board] for Tommy, Sean and Mike; it's the first time around for me," says Ciaran.

"We all know we're here to do a job. We're not here to see what the business can do for us; it's what we have to do for the business. It won't happen without effort. We all know where we stand. If something happened to one of us, the business would move forward and carry on, but in a different way."

4 TOM EHRET

SUBSEA MOGUL

TOM EHRET

FACTFILE

Name	Tom Ehret
Company	Stolt Offshore
Company Turnover	$1.5 billion
Current position	CEO
Place of birth	France
Education	Engineering degree (mechanical) – ENSAM/Paris
First job	R&D Engineer, Comex
Best business decision	Acquisition of Santa Fe's construction assets in 1989
Worst business decision	Accepting to stay for one year with acquiror of CSO in 2002 after completion of the acquisition
Which company in the upstream oil and gas industry do you admire and why?	Schlumberger: their strength is based on technology; their technology is based on a vision, on long-term planning, on R&D
Biggest dislike of the industry	The adversarial relationship between excessively strong – and increasingly bureaucratic – oil company clients and often excessively weak contractors who are regularly trapped by the cyclical nature of our business
Advice to anyone considering a career in the oil industry	Think technology first; then get around the world and work in the field: the opportunities will come
What do you think of management gurus?	Not a lot!
Favourite pastime	Reading
Favourite book	The latest crime novel from Elizabeth George
Who or what is your inspiration?	My late father who was born an orphan during WW1, fought through WW2, created a real family and had to start all over again at well over 50 after losing his job and did so joyfully and successfully
Any further ambitions?	Plenty! First make Stolt Offshore the contractor of choice in the subsea industry
Favourite quote/saying	"If you do not do everything you can, to become or remain the best, you will not be second, but you will fall to the bottom of the pile" (free translation of Marshall Lyautey's words – High Commission of Morocco in the early XX Century)

TOM EHRET

SUBSEA MOGUL

The offshore industry would not be where it is today without the incredible contribution of underwater contractors. They're a special breed and the sector today is dominated by Europe and the US. Indeed, it is generally accepted that European companies such as Stolt Offshore, Subsea 7, Technip and Saibos lead the subsea field.

Subsea today is no longer dominated by diver-based operations; rather it is a world of sophisticated ships, remotely controlled and autonomous robot vehicles, specialist tools and subsea production technologies of mind-boggling complexity to the layperson.

As with anything to do with the offshore industry, it is stuffed full of characters – strong people who know their own minds – and one such individual is French-born Tom Ehret, CEO at Stolt Offshore. He's been in the industry for 30 years thus far.

Like so many people within this remarkable industry, he landed in it quite by chance having first read for a degree in mechanical engineering. Arguably, it was only because he took an in-fill job with the famous French diving and underwater technologies company Comex, that he landed in the sector at all.

"I was due to do my national service but wasn't able to go immediately after my degree, which meant that I looked for a temporary job to earn my keep," says Ehret. "I worked as a draftsman on a day-rate basis for a few months at Comex. I ended up there by sheer accident.

"As it happened, the law changed after one year. I was then told that I didn't have to join up so I needed a real job. Comex offered me one as an engineer; that's how I ended up in the offshore industry."

But what persuaded him to become an engineer in the first place?

"As a child I always got excited about making things. I was heavily into radio, remote control and models. I had a particular aspiration for the space industry. I was dreaming of going to the moon – that was the time of the Apollo missions. I decided on being an engineer as early as 10–11 years of age. It was always clear to me that I wanted to be an engineer.

"But my being an engineer now is a bit of a fallacy as I only worked truly as one for five or six years and then I became a manager.

"But, though I haven't been doing any engineering for 30 years or so, I keep that element of general understanding of what makes things happen in this industry – engineering is the language. As an engineer in a corporate world now so driven by accountants, it becomes very handy."

At Comex, Ehret worked in a research and development hot-house that even then was focused on deepwater.

"I was working for a very famous company. With Jacques Cousteau (arguably the most famous French diver of all) to the fore on the television, there was the American space programme, it was an incredibly inspiring period," he recalls.

"One of the jobs I held during that period was with Comex SEAL (Subsea Equipment Associates Limited). It had been created by BP, Total, Westinghouse, SEP (Société Européenne de Propulsion), which has the French Arianne rocket, and others.

"There was deepwater technology, space technology, electronics – all coming together under SEAL. The remit of that organisation was to develop subsea production technology. It developed the first subsea system in the North Sea, which was installed in Mobil's Beryl field (well 9/13–1). I remember it well, I was on the job.

"It was a paradise time – almost too much so as we spent lots of money and eventually those counting the money told us to stop."

Ehret was then transferred to the US to work on various projects out of global oil capital Houston. But then he was headhunted for FMC where he became a project engineer in the group's R&D division. Importantly, Ehret came into contact and worked with a lot of Norwegians, developing systems for testing in Norway. This was the start of the Norway dimension that has since played a huge part in the Frenchman's life.

His career path in FMC was classic. Bright, quick on the uptake, Ehret climbed the ladder rapidly, leading to an assignment to Europe where he became head of product sales, later joining the top management team of FMC Europe. Success indeed, but Ehret initially railed at the very idea of being pulled off R&D and switched to sales: "When I was told that I was going to be made sales and marketing manager I was shocked – horrified. I was insulted. 'How dare they. I'm an engineer, a man of numbers and facts and figures and reality. I'm not going into this bullshit merchant role of sales and marketing.' But I wasn't given much of a choice.

"I have to admit that I enjoyed it tremendously. One wasn't just a salesman as it was about selling technology. If you were not able to understand technical issues and practical problems and talk technically with people, you couldn't sell anything.

"It was in fact a logical progression, evolving from engineering *per se* to sales and marketing with a heavy sales and marketing overlay. I was fortunate that I had remarkable bosses – individuals with vision and from whom I learned a great deal.

"The guy who managed that transition for me from engineer/researcher to marketing was Jacques Cosmao. He was CEO of FMC Europe.

"He was a really great guy – an articulate and intelligent man. I might be wrong, but at the time he took a liking to me; he was at a stage in his career where he was perhaps a little bored. I think it amused him to teach me. I was about 30, full of energy and ambition and drive and was probably a pain in the arse."

Take it on the chin

The FMC chapter closed in 1982 when Henry Delauze, founder of Comex, contacted Ehret, saying: "You used to work for me. You were a good young engineer, then you went to the Americans. They're pretty good at management and you must have learned a lot of tricks from them. Now you have learned those tricks I'd like you back."

The assignment was to become MD of Comex's North Sea joint venture with UK group Houlder Offshore – Comex Houlder Diving – out of Aberdeen.

"He pushed and shoved and charmed my wife and all the rest of it and I said yes," recalls Ehret. "He used all the tricks in the book."

The year was 1982 and the next 13 years were to be spent in the Granite City, as it is otherwise traditionally known. The business was modest at the time and hinged a lot around two semi-submersible dive support vessels – *Uncle John* and *Stadive*. However, Ehret got things moving, the company doubled in size over the next three going on four years and a new support vessel, *Aurelia*, was ordered.

But then came the 1986 oil price crash: the bottom fell out of the North Sea market and Ehret's world.

"Things got extremely tough for everyone and we were no exception, with some contracts cancelled overnight.

"I'll never forget being called on by one oil company manager in Aberdeen and he said to me: 'Look, in the 1970s the boot was on the other foot. We needed you guys, you could name your price, we had no choice and we paid. Today, the boot's on our foot. We have no money so we're not going to pay you. We're going to cancel the contracts.'

"He looked at me and said: 'So take it on the chin like a man.'

"This guy was actually pulling the rug from underneath my feet. This was the biggest customer I had – life or death for the company.

"I was so angry that I responded rudely, mixing my metaphors, and said: 'I will remember this and when the boot's on the other foot again I'll ram it up your arse sideways.'

"We were not the best of friends!"

Ehret describes the post-crash period as dreadful, but that it probably taught him more as a manager than when growing the business. This was the hard knocks school of management – learning on the hoof.

As an aside, he has never had formal management education other than several two-day sessions while at FMC. But he has been lucky several times by working for bosses or people who he says were very good at transferring their experience and knowledge.

"I've never seen anything like it. The business stopped almost instantly. Within days, projects were cancelled and, in order to survive this, I unfortunately had to lay off people and cut, cut, cut everywhere. But this is part of the game and I stuck with it.

"When we started to emerge from the crisis in 1987 I felt that Comex Houlder was too small and our balance sheets were too thin – there was hardly anything left. Might a strategic tie-up with another company be the way forward?

"I then convinced Delauze to discuss a merger with 2W (Wharton Williams Taylor) as Malcolm Williams and Rick Wharton were prepared to exit. I worked this one and in late 1987/early 1988 we pulled together a merger between Comex worldwide and Wharton Williams Taylor, which was by then a Halliburton company.

"It was an extremely interesting negotiation because you had on the one hand a very French entrepreneur, very volatile character; on the other a really professional American organisation; and, in the middle, a couple of British entrepreneurs, Rick and Malcolm, who had been with Comex in the 1970s and it turned out that there was no love lost between those two and Delauze because of the past.

"This was a period when I learned quite a bit of diplomacy in order to get this crowd to sing from the same sheet."

Eventually a merger was agreed and the different business units in Aberdeen gathered together, with some people laid off. But then the Piper Alpha tragedy occurred on 6 July 1988 when 167 offshore personnel died in a massive platform explosion. There was a silver cloud to this for Ehret in that the merger meant he was in a position to be able to deliver enough ships, welding spreads and other equipment to assist in dealing with the aftermath of what remains the worst offshore tragedy ever.

However, in late 1988, many months into a merged organisation, the lawyers had failed to tie up all the loose ends and, late one night, Ehret took a phone call that again changed the course of his career.

Break the company apart!

"I get this weird call close to midnight. It's Henry telling me: 'You know, I've had enough. I've just fallen out with these Americans. Take the whole thing apart tomorrow morning and set the company up again. You've never let me down, I have a lot of trust in you, I'm sure you'll do it alright. Good night, have a nice sleep!'

"He hung up.

"I stood there wondering whether I'd been having a nightmare. I could hardly believe what I'd heard. In the morning, I went into the office and met with my closest colleagues. We looked at one another in absolute dismay as we had been getting on really well. They had received similar calls. We had to break the company apart!

"But then, and this is not something that you can invent, my phone rings. I was sitting there with these two guys. It's a head hunter. I put him off because I wasn't in the mood to listen.

"As I hung up the phone, one of my colleagues says: 'I'm sure that guy's recruiting for Dan Olsen.'"

Olsen, a Norwegian, was the owner of the shipping group Stena, which had gone into the offshore industry in the late 1980s by buying struggling British Underwater Engineering (BUE).

"I never knew whether this head hunter was actually head hunting or not. But, since I personally knew Dan Olsen from other circumstances I thought I'd give him a ring.

"So I did, saying, 'Look, you don't necessarily know why I'm calling', because the information wasn't yet public that the merger wasn't going to happen, 'but you have several times indicated that you'd be interested in working with me. Right now I may be able to say yes, but I would come together with a couple of colleagues. Are you interested?'

"Olsen said: 'I'm jumping on a plane.'

"So he comes across, we have a discussion and we make a deal. So I quit Comex; my two colleagues, Derek Leach and Steve Davey, quit and we moved to Stena Offshore as it was then known to try and get it out of its difficulties at that time.

"When I called Henry Delauze to tell him it was over, I broke down in tears – I think I'm quite an emotional guy. However, I'm from Alsace which is culturally close to Germany and I would say that, just out of cultural heritage, we're less Gallic, less demonstrative, less volatile than the true French. I'm more North European.

"The other thing is that I left France in 1976, shortly after graduating and I lived and worked in London, Houston and Aberdeen for most of the time. So I've modified my behaviour to be more acceptable! To blend in better."

By 1990, Ehret had Stena Offshore on an even keel and the oil companies were finally plucking up courage to reinvest after the '86 crash. He describes the next few years as fantastic and attributes a great deal of the success to the way in which he was treated by Olsen.

Olsen – masterful leader

"Now there you're really talking about a very unassuming person. You wouldn't believe for one second that this man was such a powerful person.

"He was a fine individual, extremely low key. He really worked with manage-ment – me and my colleagues. It was absolutely fantastic – I learned so much.

"Dan Olsen used to call me every morning of every day of every week at around seven o'clock. We would chat, just chat. He would say: 'What's up, what are you going to tackle today.'

"He was completely non-directive. It was a chat. It was exchanging, massaging material. It wasn't directing me, it wasn't requesting, it wasn't anything like that, it was just talking. It was quite an extraordinary way of giving me confidence while, at the same time, by talking directly, putting me under pressure. It worked very well. We had a fantastic relationship."

But it wasn't always that way.

"I'll never forget, after a few months, when things were still pretty tough, we had a board meeting. I presented a budget and Dan was not happy with it. He was expecting to see much bigger numbers, so he was quite negative about what I was saying. I got quite shirty about it. He was very unpleasant for a while. Then the meeting was over and we all head off, in my case home.

"That night, lying in bed, I couldn't sleep. Two or three o'clock in the morning I'd had enough. I got up and drove to the office at Westhill (a satellite of Aberdeen). I sat in my office, it was dark, cold, and suddenly my phone rings.

"I'm thinking, who the hell would call me at three in the morning; must be my wife realising that I'd gone. I pick up the phone. It's Dan Olsen. 'I take it you couldn't sleep. I couldn't sleep either,' he says.

"We had this surreal chat at three in the morning – he in a London hotel being unable to sleep because he was unhappy about our having had a fight and me being unhappy for the same reason. So we chatted, got over our differences and moved on. An extraordinary man!

"He could have acted in a much more forceful way, but he used a very soft method of taking people along."

As Stena Offshore increasingly prospered, the parent Stena Group was making heavy weather and in crisis by 1993, having bought Sealink, formerly part of British Rail. Dan Olsen and his board came under growing pressure to cash in Stena Offshore.

At that stage, a number of companies made attempts to buy the business, McDermott being one; Herrema and Allseas were two others. Ehret admits to being angry at the time.

"There I was, with my team, we had turned things around, we had worked bloody hard and, just as we were getting to a position of some success, some stability, we were about to be taken out by people who I felt wouldn't bring anything to us and would in fact destroy our success.

"I had a discussion with Dan Olsen about it and then went back to him with a management buy-out proposal. That was an interesting experience. We didn't have any money, but we managed to get institutional support and we were seriously considering making an offer.

"But Dan told me that he liked me too much to accept. He said: 'If I accept this, you're going to be so heavily in debt for the rest of your life, it's going to be terrible for you. I know you, you already work so hard; you'll kill yourself. So I don't accept your offer. It would be a bad thing to do to a friend.'

"But he and I agreed that we would try and take the company public, which was one way for shareholders to exit without the company being taken over. So we headed for the States and tried to get into an initial public offering situation."

Stena Offshore's top team were ready to go to the market in 1994. This was a US city-hopping marathon – six o'clock in the morning starts, doing several cities in a day using a small helicopter.

Ehret had success within his grasp, but then Alan Greenspan made a key speech announcing that he would increase the US base rate by half a point; furthermore, there would be more interest rises to come. Reaction was swift, with some of those committed to buying stock pulling out and, within 24 hours, he no longer had a deal.

"We went home with our tails between our legs feeling very tired and sorry for ourselves, at which point I proposed another solution, namely to merge Stena Offshore with French company Coflexip because Coflexip had in fact made an IPO successfully about six months before our attempt.

"They used the same bank, they were the same size, they had similar possibilities. We were in a similar business, they just had better timing. They had succeeded whereas we had failed. So I suggested that we merged with them and acquire a public listing that way.

"We entered into negotiations and eventually did it; as a result of that we formed CSO – Coflexip Stena Offshore."

War in the boardroom

It was a difficult negotiation because this was a cross-border merger and such arrangements frequently fail. The fact that Ehret was French was initially thought to be a plus as there would be no need for a go-between.

A deal was sealed, Ehret was named chief operating officer and Christian Marbach became chairman/CEO because he was in his late 50s/early 60s whereas Ehret was in his early 40s.

Everyone though they would get on well. The problem was that Coflexip was quite French, Marbach was very French and Ehret was not as French as they thought. They really didn't get on at all.

"The guy was a former civil servant," recalls Ehret. "We were on different pages. It was not going to work even though I tried hard for many months.

"The Coflexip side was in conquering mode; this was not a merger of equals. We all know mergers of equals don't exist because one is always more equal than the other and they were definitely feeling a lot more equal than us.

"There was conflict – 1995 was a horrible year. At the end I had had enough. I was still a board member as well as COO and I did something that, today, I probably would not do. I wrote a letter to the other board members wherein I stated politely that the company was going to run into difficulties if the board didn't make up their minds as to how they wanted the company to be run. There were two different styles, two different methods, two different directions. They had to choose one.

"That was extremely unwise on my part. As one of the other directors told me: 'Why the hell did you write this, now we're going to have to act because it's a written document and we can't leave it without acting.'

"It got very nasty, there was a fight and the French system got involved. In France, senior civil servants are part of the establishment – what the French call corps. There was a lot of lobbying at board level – from government, the oil company Elf, and so on.

"They closed ranks. But I had a lot of support from Dan Olsen, who was still on the board and owned about 30% of the joint company. He told them: 'If Tom Ehret goes, I'm dumping my 30% on the market tomorrow morning.' That got their attention."

Thus emerged a typical Gallic compromise. Ehret was asked to step down from the board and to resign as COO, but allowed to remain in the company. Marbach was asked to leave and he was replaced by Pierre Marie Valentin, who was in his 60s and a well-known company doctor. He had saved another French underwater contractor, Technip, from bankruptcy in the 1980s and Ehret was asked to work with him.

"I remember, he [Valentin] and I sat down over dinner the night before all of this was to unfold. I was dejected, pissed off and I told him that I was going to be on my bike. He said: 'Don't do that, give me three months, I really need your help. Work with me and you won't regret it.'

"He cleared out a lot of Coflexip management and very strongly pulled the two companies together. He did a fantastic job without a doubt. He asked me to stay, saying: 'You're going to be COO again. Let's forget what happened and work together.'"

What Valentin did was to punish those who played politics while working with those who may have had strong opinions, may have been writing letters like Ehret had, but wanted the good of the company.

"He was a very hard, difficult person. He wanted nothing less than perfection in everything. He was permanently criticising and screaming. He was a very tough boss. I have to admit that, while I didn't like it every day, I learned a great deal from the guy, especially in what I can best describe as pure management.

"All of us have to be competent in what we do, but to be a leader you have to pay attention to everything in the smallest detail, you have to communicate intensively all the time. You have to be mindful of the fact that everything you say, every attitude you take, is going to be watched and interpreted. If you're not careful, you may send a wrong signal."

Polishing his performance

Thanks to Valentin, Ehret was beginning to acquire some polish and, working together, it appears that CSO did well, especially on the US financial market. Performance was reflected in the share price and the best multiple in the subsea business for a long time.

Acquisitions were made, the last being Aker Deepwater in 2000 for $625 million. This turned CSO into the leader in its class worldwide.

Just ahead of that deal, Stena still had 30% of the shares in CSO and decided to sell. At the time there were a number of potential buyers for that share and the keenest was Technip. As noted earlier, Technip was the company that Valentin had turned around in the 1980s. He could see that if Technip bought Stena's 30% share, Technip would be in a perfect position to effect a complete takeover in the fullness of time and create what he called the French Halliburton. Before retiring he wanted to bring these two companies together and indeed a deal was done – a so-called amicable full offer.

But Ehret had a different view: "I did not share his enthusiasm for the French Halliburton. But I'm a disciplined person so I did what I had to do. Since he was retiring, Valentin asked me to chair the committee of the board that was negotiating with Technip in order to get our equity shareholders the best possible deal, which we did.

"We obtained 199 euros per share at a time when the share price was in the 160 euros range. We got a very good deal – I had no disgruntled shareholders out there. But, it is true to say that, throughout that fight, I didn't make any friends at Technip, which is understandable, I suppose."

After completion of this deal in 2002, Valentin became non-executive chairman of the supervisory board and Ehret became vice-chair of the management board of which Technip's Daniel Valot was appointed chairman. The five-strong top team comprised three Technip and two CSO seniors. The CSO pair were Ehret and colleague Pierre Girot. But the arrangement failed and Girot left pretty quickly. He didn't like the set-up, according to Ehret, who was now on his own; having promised a year as his part of the CSO–Technip bargain, he did so, then left.

Back-tracking to the negotiations in the mid-90s, it was at this time that Ehret received a phonecall from a certain banker on behalf of Jacob Stolt-Nielsen of Norwegian underwater contractor Stolt Offshore.

"Said the banker: 'He asked me to call you because he would like you to consider becoming CEO of Stolt Offshore.'

"At the time I said 'I'm far too busy right now – I'm involved in some other transaction that I can't tell you anything about. I'm not on the market, but thanks very much – have a nice day.'"

That was that, or so Ehret thought. But a few months later, towards the end of 2002, Jacob Stolt-Nielsen was back on the phone and Ehret was more receptive. He was offered the job of CEO at Stolt Offshore.

"He caught my attention as I was by then keen to find a new challenge, so I accepted, made the jump and joined Stolt Offshore in March 2003.

"Again it's almost back to the future because in Stolt Offshore I found something of Comex because Stolt had acquired Comex in 1991 to create Stolt Comex Seaway.

"I found some of my former colleagues. It was quite amusing. Some of the guys that work with me now, I used to work with in the 1970s. It really is a small world – it's good fun.

"I joined ostensibly to help the company recover from difficult times and I guess the rest is public knowledge. It's been quite tough work. As a result of past mistakes, of past losses, Jacob Stolt-Nielsen and Stolt-Nielsen Group eventually exited from Stolt Offshore and so has become a fully traded company.

"We are 100% quoted on NASDAQ and the Oslo bourse. We have about 45% of our shareholders in the US and 55% in Europe. In the European portion, about half is in UK and the other half between Scandinavia and Germany."

Gone back into the pampas

Why has Ehret (now London-based) taken on so many difficult jobs in an industry that has been to hell and back again at least twice since the dawn of North Sea oil?

The answer: "I don't know. I'm generally regarded as someone who has been quite determined. I guess it goes back to the way I was educated. My father used to say when we were kids: 'Remember son, obstacles in your way are just there for you to surmount. Never give up.'

"There again, a lot of people have told me over the years: 'You pratt, why do you keep at it? Haven't you done enough? Why don't you do something with less stress?'

"For instance, I could have stayed at Technip. I was vice-chairman of the management board, president of Technip Offshore, I was well paid, I had a big black car that I could park in front of the building like the chairman and I was, being in the French system, impossible to remove. It would have taken a shareholder motion to remove me from my job.

"Some said to me: 'You must be nuts to leave this and go to run a company in difficulty. Why do you do it?'

"And you know, in a way it's very simple. I felt old. I felt drained, I felt there was no fun in being that big shot in a big traditional French company.

"Henry Delauze said to me on the phone, because he rang me after he had heard that I was going to move. 'So, you've picked up your spurs, jumped on your horse, and gone back into the pampas.'

"It's a colourful way of putting it, if you will. I guess I need the challenge, the buzz, I also need the teamwork.

"Right now, here at Stolt Offshore, ask the top team of people who have been with me through Stena Offshore, Coflexip Stena, Technip. They've joined me time and time again, not because I'm a hero but because I think we work well together as a team.

"It's the only type of work that I think is adequate for this type of business. When you put as much of yourself as much as I and these guys do, you don't want to do so in an environment that is cold, rigid, unfriendly. You want to do it in an environment that's fun.

"You want to be able to go to the pub with the lads and have a good session. You want to be able to yell at one another yet not feel angry. You want to be able to argue everything. You want to be able to get that daily buzz of achieving things, making a difference, not administering in a very proper manner from behind a big desk – a large empire – a different story, you know."

Pause for thought

"I have a message for students and it is to first be themselves. I don't think there are recipes. I don't believe there are do's and don'ts.

"Be yourself, believe in yourself, believe that you have something to contribute and do it with your whole heart and soul and your gut. Don't look for a model, don't look for recipes, don't look for the perfect way of getting to the top. That's bullshit. I believe in honesty and ethic. In the long run, up-front people always win. Those who make it through are those who are believers in what they do, that are honest with what they do. They are looking to get the best out of the company; not some ulterior motive.

"Secondly, don't let politics pollute your life. Be sincere – be honest. Ethic must rank high if you want to be someone – to look in the mirror and be happy.

"The third point is work hard. Work ethic has pretty much disappeared in some quarters. Not so much in this country [UK], but certainly France is one where work ethic has been bashed for the past 25 years, where everyone has been hammering work is evil, the less work you do the better off you are, you have the right not to do anything, blah, blah, blah. Youngsters might believe this stuff. I don't.

Have a work ethic – do things well. It can be the most menial task, but do it well. And respect the work of others, because work is life, energy – they put themselves into it.

5 JOHN KENNEDY

TOP DRAWER MOGUL

JOHN KENNEDY

FACTFILE

Name	John William Kennedy
Company	Vetco International plus Wellstream International
Company turnover	$1.9 billion (2004) and $180 million (2004) respectively
Current position	Executive Chairman, Vetco International; Chairman, Wellstream
Place of birth	Dublin, Ireland
Education	Bachelor of Engineering (electrical) – University College, Dublin London Business School – Sloan fellowship programme – gained MSc in Finance
First job	Schlumberger – wireline engineer
Best business decision	To establish and invest in a technical training and personnel development programme at Dresser Atlas
Worst business decision	To leave the technical sphere
Which company in the upstream oil and gas industry do you admire and why?	BP – very performance-driven culture
Biggest dislike of the industry	Travel
Advice to anyone considering a career in the oil industry?	Follow your dream, be persistent, apply yourself. Despite what people say, there's no substitute for hard work and long hours
What do you think of management gurus?	They have their role – always informative but should never be accepted as a creed
Favourite pastime	Golf, shooting
Favourite book	Anything by Winston S. Churchill
Who or what is your inspiration?	My family – always supportive, always encouraging, allowed me to do what I needed to do, including travelling away from home for weeks on end
Any further ambitions?	I want to continue to develop companies in the oil and gas business
Favourite quote/saying	You don't know what you don't know

JOHN KENNEDY

TOP DRAWER MOGUL

In January 2004, troubled Swiss-Swedish engineering giant ABB completed the sale of most of its oil and gas business to a syndicate comprising Candover, NIB Partners, JP Morgan Partners and 3i for $924 million. It was the biggest supply chain acquisition that year and ended 24 months of uncertainty for some 7,500 employees across 31 countries. Not that ABB had been running the business down: investment in new plant and machinery was sustained throughout the two years with the result that the syndicate undoubtedly picked up a first-class operation.

Appointed to the role of executive chairman was high-flying Irishman, John Kennedy, a former vice-president at Halliburton, one of the world's largest energy services multinationals. This was the second chairmanship that Candover had offered to Kennedy in less than a year as, in March 2003, he became non-exec chairman of oilfield pipeline technologies specialist Wellstream, after Halliburton sold the company to a grouping led by Candover for $136 million. At the same time, he was also asked by the private equity house to assist in identifying future targets.

"They wanted to establish a presence in the energy field but didn't want to go with the exploration and production side," says Kennedy. "They wanted oil services and felt that it was a good point in terms of the valuation side. I became their adviser."

It would be reasonable to say that Candover and its partners probably hit the jackpot. Kennedy sums it up well: "How often does an opportunity like this come along. It's a recipe made in heaven. You don't get better."

More later of Vetco International and how this quintessential Irishman is taking the group forward. But what is it about Kennedy that has enabled him to get to the very top of the international oil and gas supply chain, for to have been a VP at Halliburton is exactly that?

His was a classic start – read for a degree in electrical engineering at University College Dublin and straight into Schlumberger (an arch rival of Halliburton in many respects) that happened to be on a trawl for talent in Ireland.

"They came on the milk round; I liked them and joined aged 20 to seek my fortune; it was as simple as that.

"At Schlumberger there was rather strict on-job training where you have to pass exams at regular intervals. Though most is on-the-job, you are started off by being sent to a training school for about five months – in my case Holland – where you learn all there is to know about wireline engineering [a particular type of oil and gas well servicing system] and petrophysics. It was then about a year in Great Yarmouth, about six–nine months in Aberdeen and then nearly two years in Saudi Arabia. At Schlumberger you didn't have a choice, you were very definitely told what you're going to do."

It was a hot-house environment designed to get the intellectual and practical best out of people like Kennedy.

"I think, from the Schlumberger point of view, the thing you learn very quickly is that you're on your own and you get a lot of responsibility very early. I think you develop and learn personal independence, to think on your own, to be rather self-sufficient mentally because, as a young man, you're going out on a rig, running a wireline unit and you've got to be fairly self-sufficient."

But, after five years, and by then a senior engineer, he says he got fed up with travelling and wanted to return to Europe. It was 1977.

"A friend of mine knew of a job going at Dresser Atlas [an American company but with a European presence]: he told them about me, they made contact, I was eager, so it went from there. I joined as a petro-physicist and I think that's where I began to learn my people skills. It was a rather small organisation and I guess natural ambition drove me onwards to do the things I did while there. I just wanted to get on in life."

Face that fits

The first job in at Dresser Atlas in fact saw Kennedy sent to Houston for six months of training before returning to Europe and opening a computer centre which he ran for a year. But his real desire was to get close to the customer and spark off in a way that, arguably, few can do as well as the Irish.

"I always had a great personal need to be close to the customer, deriving a lot of pleasure of dealing face to face. I think Dresser Atlas probably recognised that and, rather surprisingly, in 1979, they made me sales manager for Europe, Africa and Middle East."

However, two years later he was back in Houston at Dresser Atlas HQ to take up a senior posting – managing planning activities for the corporation's oilfield services group.

"Intellectually that was very important for my career – learning to produce work of a certain standard at an executive level that I wouldn't normally have had to do at that age. I did that for about a year and then they sent me back to Europe as general manager Europe, Africa and the Middle East."

Basically, Kennedy was on an escalator and could do no wrong. In 1987 he was promoted to executive VP at Dresser Atlas and a year later he became president and CEO. In 1993 he was made president, Dresser Drilling & Production Services (1993); then president/CEO of then new Dresser creation Kellogg Oil & Gas (1995); and finally president, Dresser Enterprises (1997). He led the company into its merger with Halliburton in 1998 to create an energy services giant whose turnover topped $16 billion a year at the time.

Clearly gifted, Kennedy had made it to the top of the Dresser tree, but how did he do it?

"It was simple, I just worked all the hours that God gave. I really liked doing what I did for all those years. I remember one time saying to my wife in the 1980s: 'Is there anyone as happy as me? I really love getting up in the morning and driving to the office. I really love the job.' I was only 38 when I was made group president of Dresser."

Kennedy had been lucky: he started out with a decent degree and had been on the receiving end of excellent schooling since, both at Schlumberger and Dresser. He determined that this should become a core aspect of Dresser life.

"I really saw a huge business advantage in setting up a training school and training people. We were very aggressively recruiting in universities and developing our own people because I really believed in that and I really believe that young people should get the same chances to advance as I got and really push them forward and give them early responsibility as quickly as possible. They all responded very positively and the organisation grew on the back of that.

"My boss Jack Murphy, the chairman of Dresser at the time, was a great mentor and he had always wanted me to do the Harvard executive courses and we thought it was a great time in my career to go and do an MBA. In the end I went and did the MSc in finance in London. That gave a skill-set I had not previously had in terms of analysing financial information. I went back into the business late 1992."

Ask Kennedy why he thinks Jack Murphy took a shine to him and the response is: "Put bluntly, I suppose it was because I produced the results. For example, when we set Dresser Atlas up in Europe we went from a very meagre to very material market share of about 25% in about seven years."

And why did Kennedy take a shine to Murphy?

"I guess it was his approachability; he was someone who gave you the opportunity, licence to get on and do things."

Mentoring and things

Is Kennedy a mentor?

"I used to have what I call development training. When I was in Dresser I set up a group for high performers where we picked guys that showed promise and rotated them quickly to different jobs.

"I've always had a very open-door policy for that type of person, where they could come along and talk with you and where you can be fairly open and blunt with them and help them along in their career. I think you have to provide that sort of thing. You have to engender an ethical approachability within the organisation and you have to allow people to marry their personal horizons with their professional horizons – they're always very much inter-linked.

"One of the things that someone told me some time ago is that you have to look upon the business as a family. You're dealing with a daddy, brother, sister, not just an employee. I think it beholds you to respect that situation. That can be achieved even in companies as large as Dresser or Halliburton. You have to implicitly respect.

"I always look upon business as, this is not the army, it's an elective situation. If you don't treat people properly they don't have to stay around. They can leave. So you have to make it worth their while professionally and personally to stay with you.

"I think that one's role as a leader is basically to provide two things: one is vision to engender a sense of confidence in people and the second is a licence to allow people to perform. You have to allow them to make mistakes with some degree of impunity.

"Once they learn from them and get on, you've got to provide that sort of operational framework where people have a licence to perform, to try something, to be successful and feel successful in their own right."

Returning to Kennedy's climb to the all-but-pinnacle of the global oil and gas services supply chain, the merger between Halliburton and Dresser was born of the late 1997 through 1999 oil price crisis that resulted in some of the largest mergers the world had ever witnessed – big brand oil corporations Exxon tying up with Mobil; BP with Amoco and then Atlantic Richfield; Chevron with Texaco; and Conoco with Phillips.

Kennedy admits this was a gut-wrenching period, especially since Dresser's identity was eliminated. However, his view is that the Dresser–Halliburton merger was very complementary – there wasn't a great deal of overlap. When asked as to whether Dresser-Halliburton was one of those rare examples of a merger that actually worked (most do not), Kennedy's reply is: "There was not the normal level of portfolio rationalisation – the different product lines were complementary rather than competitive."

While he had been with Dresser for more than 20 years, Kennedy clearly grasped the opportunities that the merger presented with open arms.

"I enjoyed it. I very much liked working with the people. I don't have any regrets. A lot of other people have said that they did; I didn't. I got on well with the management, including Dick Cheney [then CEO of Halliburton and now at the right hand of US President George W. Bush as Vice-President] and Halliburton president Dave Lesar. I was given a lot of opportunity."

Lasting the longest

"I think I was the Dresser executive to last the longest. I was probably the last to leave and I think I was promoted fairly dramatically from the time that I joined."

This included serving as COO of Halliburton's Brown & Root Energy Services (BRES) business unit.

The ultimate Halliburton accolade came in May 2000 when Kennedy was elevated to executive VP of Halliburton responsible for global business development. Welcoming the appointment, Lesar said at the time: "John's business experience makes him a tremendous asset to Halliburton's management team as we enhance the industry's leading suite of products and services we provide our customers."

Reference has already been made as to whether his being Irish has had any bearing on Kennedy's phenomenal climb: after all, the world is peppered with a lot of very successful Irishmen, most with that distinctively agreeable style – an ability to fit in just about anywhere. Says Kennedy: "The hindsight view is that I think there is some merit to the observation. I think that we tend to be fairly people-oriented and blend in fairly well, yet still be sufficiently visible to climb very high."

Two years later, life was about to change for Kennedy. In 2002 he was introduced to Marek Gumeinny, MD at Candover, who wanted to buy into oil and gas services – basically build a porfolio within the sector. Gumeinny offered Kennedy a piece of the action, as he judged the urbane Irishman ideally qualified because of his huge experience in the sector.

"I liked the whole concept of so doing and off we went together," recalls Kennedy. In March 2003 we bought Wellstream – a fairly big decision at the time as the market then wasn't as exciting as it is now."

Wellstream is a leading global manufacturer of flexible pipe applications for the offshore deepwater oil and gas sector and Kennedy already knew the business.

"Wellstream was a company that reported to me when I ran Kellogg Oil & Gas so I was fairly familiar with it. It had gone through management changes in the interim period. Gordon Chapman, a former CEO, was very much the guy who developed Wellstream and I suppose had done more than anyone else to make it successful. Candover backed a buy-in team led by him.

"Directly after that, we started chasing the ABB oil and gas division, and that happened in July 2004."

As executive chairman, Kennedy's job is to straighten out and home what is now known as Vetco International, which has two primary operating units: Vetco Gray and Vetco Aibel.

Vetco Gray is largely UK-based and concentrates on design, engineering, manufacture and installation of drilling and completion systems for oil and gas production infrastructure onshore, offshore and subsea.

Vetco Aibel is located in Norway and offers a complete suite of specialised hardware and software for field life support; design, engineering and assembly of modules and hydrocarbon processing facilities; and maintenance and modification services for facilities located on top of platforms and provided on a multi-year contracted basis.

Brilliant outlook

Group turnover in 2004 was $1.9 billion – on target. This should be viewed against a global market for oilfield equipment, systems and services estimated to be worth $160 billion a year and growing at 10% per annum.

Kennedy has worked fast to implement changes that he believes will help take Vetco International to the next level. Those changes include: further honing of an already highly experienced management team; manufacturing plant now operate on a global rather than regional basis, but continue to service local markets as required; a solutions-based, rather than product-based, approach has been adopted; global account management has been implemented, with individuals allocated specific oil companies to ensure there is always a familiar, friendly voice at the end of a phone; and there is tighter financial management.

"It's about being more rigorous in running the company while getting total buy-in from our customers and our own people," says Kennedy. "We have reviewed all key contracts and are trying to inject cross-learning between them. And there are lots of new contracts coming up."

On technology and cutting-edge engineering development, which is one of the hallmarks of Vetco, he says the initial preoccupation has been on "cleaning up" the portfolio of technologies offered and under development. By this, he means being clear on which technologies fit the market and where the priorities lie.

"We've inherited a number of key technologies but, in the past, not enough effort has been put into their monetisation. But let's do something exciting, something bold. Remember, we have a global footprint through which we can market such technologies, such solutions."

However, the most fundamental asset at Vetco International is its people and Kennedy is obviously very well aware of this and of the need to ensure that they don't simply walk, as did a fair number in the two years prior to the deal struck with ABB.

"They were owned by a rather distressed parent at the time. You could be cruel and say that any new home was a better one than the old home; and I think there is something in that. There was a great deal of uncertainty in these people's lives. But then along we came, bought the company, and created certainty and some level of security."

That he knew exactly what he was buying in skills terms was indicated to the author just a few weeks after the deal was concluded: "It's one of the great benefits that we see in this acquisition. By any measure, against any peer, the competence of Vetco International will establish itself as a new benchmark. The best of the other players in its sector will be a distant second."

Kennedy possesses huge self-belief and a belief in the ability of others. His simple view is that, if he can get to the top, so can most people, if they apply themselves, and that includes students.

"My own experience is that, and I really do believe it, most things in life are, within reason, achievable. It's all about personal discipline and application. If you're ready to put in the hours, most young graduates will be successful. But you have to have a rather unrestrained approach to your business life. I think that those who do that will eventually be successful."

5 LARRY KINCH

SERIAL MOGUL

LARRY KINCH

		FACTFILE
Name	Larry Kinch	
Company	EDP (Chairman) Venture Production (NXD)	
Company turnover	N/A	
Current position	EDP Chairman	
Place of birth	Aberdeen	
Education	FTC Electrical Engineering	
First job	Apprentice in industrial instrumentation	
Best business decision	To go on my own	
Worst business decision	Put too many eggs in one basket!	
Which company in the upstream oil and gas industry do you admire and why?	Shell/BP – Shell for its technical depth (despite reserves debacle); BP for the commercial insight under Lord Browne	
Biggest dislike of the industry	Conservatism, individual risk-averse attitude	
Advice to anyone considering a career in the oil industry	This is not a sunset industry; opportunity is huge for young people, in particular because of the challenge and demographics	
What do you think of management gurus?	Not a lot (most preach things they have not personally done)	
Favourite pastime	Motorsport/shooting	
Favourite book	Bios on successful people	
Who or what is your inspiration?	Churchill (Never Give Up)	
Any further ambitions?	To keep on winning	
Favourite quote/saying	Change is the only constant	

LARRY KINCH

SERIAL MOGUL

In May 2005, a novel deal was struck between Energy Development Partners (EDP) of Aberdeen and BP to enable development of two financially stranded UK onshore oilfields.

It's not because the super-major is strapped for cash; rather BP's focus is on hunting for and developing giant oil and gas fields elsewhere in the world. Until EDP stepped into the frame, the Wareham and Kimmeridge fields in Dorset were marginal and candidates for selling off.

Instead, a partnering arrangement has been forged whereby EDP is pumping money and expertise into the project in return for a slice of the returns, while BP retains ownership. Moreover, the contract is "generic", meaning that if this arrangement works, the energy major will offer further similarly stranded assets for EDP to work. It could be described as a symbiotic relationship where both parties ultimately benefit.

EDP expects to reach similar agreements with other oil companies on a similar basis. And, if these come to fruition, then it would mean the firm investing some $250 million, plus specialist expertise, over the period 2005–08 – but the sum could be considerably higher.

Catalyst to this imaginative way of doing business is oilfield entrepreneur Larry Kinch, who devised the EDP concept in early 2002 and launched it in September 2003. But behind the bold idea are many years of experience as a North Sea new ventures pioneer, and a paper round in a wealthy district of Aberdeen.

"I'm a great believer in the Freudian concept that a child is formed by its environment – where it's been brought up," says Kinch. "It gives you a hunger if you're brought up in an environment where you understand the only way forward is to actually do it yourself.

"In sport, you see many young people from poor backgrounds viewing their passion as the only way out and they become world champions. The hunger is there. It's not that dissimilar a situation for a lot of entrepreneurs.

"When I was being brought up there was always plenty of food on the table, clothes on my back and a bed to sleep in, but there weren't the luxuries that, for example, my children have."

The son of a Canadian soldier who fought in World War II and an Aberdeen mother, Kinch was raised in council houses, first in the city's Mastrick district and then Garthdee. That alone was a powerful incentive.

"I was about 10 or 12 years old when I realised that, if I wanted these things, I had to go out and achieve them. In fact I started a paper round when I was nine, not the normal 13.

"It gave me a level of financial independence. My parents were great, they helped me where they could but they didn't have the means to back some of the things I wanted to get into. I was deeply involved in cycling when I was a youth. Even then buying a top of the range cycle was hundreds of pounds – a hand-built Mercian. I think I paid £150 for it in 1967.

"I used to have a paper round doing the bigger houses in the smart suburbs of Pitfodels and Cults. Some had exotic names and I dreamed of the people who'd made their fortune in the days of the British Empire and returned. I decided that I would do that too – some day.

"I also delivered what they called extras – pamphlets that you poked through people's doors – Spar – one penny off your tatties. The objective was to make money.

"In those days you also collected the paper money and you often got tips. You soon learned a bit of courtesy and civility – that's what got the tips."

Kinch got out of school when he was 16, straight into an engineering apprenticeship, sponsored by the now defunct Culter paper mill where his father worked.

None of the family had ever gone to university, so that wasn't on the agenda. A pity perhaps as Kinch's school performance was good. However, the convention was get out of school soonest, get a job, get married.

Bright streak

The bright streak showed through at the mill, with the result that he was offered a new apprenticeship in instrument engineering because there was more automation coming into paper at that time (1969). And it was back into education, doing a Higher National Diploma in electrical engineering on day release/evening classes as part of the training.

At that time, Kinch started to pursue a passion, a really serious passion that endures today through a stable of some of the world's finest road and track machines.

"I had already developed a fascination for cars but the only way I could afford one was to get an old wreck and rebuild it. I started in Jaguars, which was probably my first entrepreneurial venture. At that time a Ford Escort was the goal, but so many people wanted one that you had to pay perhaps £30 for an engine from a scrap yard, whereas no one wanted an old Jag and they'd mostly give the engine away too. They were more expensive to run, but it was far cheaper to acquire the bits."

As with every other individual in this book, the dawn of North Sea oil was to have a profound impact. In his case, Kinch completed his apprenticeship and married just before his 20th birthday, having met his wife Ann when they were both 17. They landed on their feet.

"We were lucky as my job at Culter mill was deemed critical – I was on 24-hour call because of the automation and was given a house by the mill – a lovely granite building overlooking the river Dee. That was fantastic for a 19-year old."

By then, the mill was in trouble having been hit by soaring oil prices as its systems were oil-fired. When crude tripled in price during the early 1970s, this put the mill on the back-foot and tied-houses such as the Kinch residence were sold to the city council. Kinch took this as a cue to get out of paper. Instead he hit the North Sea klondike trail along with thousands of others, in his case landing a job with Schlumberger, initially as a service engineer.

"The week I went through my first interview in Aberdeen there were 250 such interviews of applicants from all over the world. They were held at an industrial unit in Dyce in batches of about 20 a day. The interview started at 8am, you got no lunch, though you got a sandwich and can of beer at 2pm. Over that time you were examined in English, maths and aptitude. Then at 4pm, everyone was told the time of their one-to-one interviews.

"I was told I would be last, because I lived locally. I complained bitterly about that because there was something I wanted to watch on telly that night. So I ended up having an argument. The guy said: 'When you're with Schlumberger, you'll do as you're told.'

"Having put in eight hours to that point I bit my tongue and decided I would miss the programme. I was one of only six selected out of that 250. There were guys much better academically qualified than me, but I had practical skills on my side."

"Flew to Paris for a medical – first time I'd been on a plane – the medical was held at a place on Rue Colonel Drion. You got a certificate from them that declared: 'fit for tropical service'."

Three months' induction followed, then Kinch was ready for action.

"Of course, my first tropical service was the North Sea – exploration well testing from semi-submersible rigs in Denmark, Norway and the UK. That was early 1974 – the place was booming. My very first assignment was to the Bluewater III, an old American semi-submersible rig, appraisal well testing on the Argyll field discovery (the first UK oilfield into commercial production). The operator was Signal Oil & Gas.

"I basically spent the next couple of years working in the North Sea until I joined Shell as an instrument engineer in 1976. That included a six weeks' induction course at which I contradicted the person who was lecturing everyone about the services that Schlumberger provided. He requested a word with me at the end of the meeting – I thought I was in for a bollocking.

I love Shell

"He asked what department I was in. I said engineering. He asked me if I would like to transfer to well/petroleum engineering – Shell was short of people with my skills. 'That's more important to Shell than what we recruited you as,' he said."

"So I did, got an automatic job grade increase – just six weeks into the company. I loved working for Shell, we were well looked after. At that time the average guy was working one week on, one week off. But the change in role meant I was based onshore, working offshore as and when needed.

"In those couple of years with Shell in the North Sea, I probably learned more than a lot of people would learn in ten today. I was probably an oddity. Whereas the average Shell guy was climbing up the wall after seven days offshore, I was quite happy to stay two or three weeks at a time offshore.

"I was making great money: £10–12,000 a year which seemed a lot at the time; I thought I might spend my entire career with Shell.

"But, while driving to work one day, thinking I was the happiest guy around in terms of career and working for a super company, I realised I was never going to get one of those big houses along North Deeside Road by working for Shell in Aberdeen.

"I particularly wanted one of the large new bungalows that were built at that time. A quick calculation showed that I was not going to be able to afford it, so I asked Shell for an overseas posting. They said no because I was required in the North Sea. My reply was that if I couldn't do it with them, I would do it with someone else.

"Within a week I saw an advertisement; BP was looking for people to go out to Qatar. We went *en famille* – my wife Ann, daughter Melanie and baby son Elliot."

The two or three years that Kinch envisaged he would be there became eight and he resigned in 1985, by which time he was senior petroleum engineer.

"Life was good and I had bought a house in Cyprus. The intention had been to spend my career in the Middle East. But then two things happened. I saw a lot of guys in Aberdeen who had gone into business for themselves and were making a lot of money. They were good enough but I was unimpressed by their technical skills. My conclusion was that if they could do it then so can I. In any case I was significantly better qualified and experienced than they were.

"I think it is important to note too that, over prior years, I was forever on at the major service providers to improve their products and services. Many times I gave them ideas and six months later they were commercialised. I got to thinking there was a business in this.

"So I decided to go into business. Ann's response was that we were young enough – only 32, we had money behind us – about £50,000, plus we had a house in Cults by that time, so why not. But it took almost a year to extract myself from my Middle East contract with BP."

On paper, Kinch's timing seemed dreadful. The 1986 oil price crash was in full swing and the North Sea industry was hurting badly. He had surely got it wrong. But read the situation differently.

"I remember some colleagues saying I was mad. Not at all; reality is that it was the opposite. I had timed it right. I always say that this industry is at its worst when it's making a lot of money because it becomes risk averse, complacent and does things the expensive way."

And so Petroleum Engineering Services (PES) came into being.

"In 1986, my first job was with Occidental. The company had a hole in a well completion about 11,000 feet down. The economics of a well workover [overhaul] weren't there. They had been told by government officials to shut the well in as it had a 'live annulus' [gas/oil where it shouldn't be]."

First steps as an entrepreneur

"What we did, myself and my co-founder of PES, Ian McCrindle (also heritage Shell), was to design a tool that would 'pack-off' and seal the leak. It took us about eight weeks to design and build; we had no contract. I went offshore, ran the tool, it worked and all of a sudden we were heroes inside Occidental. We had saved them a $10 million well.

"Within weeks we had another interesting problem – a well that has died and there is no gas-lift point to help kick-start it. Occidental asked if we could design a tool that would enable gas-lift to be retro-fitted. We did.

"However, we didn't know how to price things. My philosophy was to ask, what kind of value does this sort of work create? So I increase the price fourfold over the price of the prior tool and they didn't flinch."

It happens that this financial innocence paid off as PES secured all of Occidental's specialist work in the North Sea.

"But it was hard work and I was very naïve. I had jumped off the aeroplane and hoped for a soft landing. The first two years were in fact very tough."

It was a period that defined Kinch for what he is today, an ideas person with a flare for technology and business innovation – indeed, an entrepreneur.

While he and McCrindle set PES up together on a 50:50 basis, Kinch says he was the one who propelled the business.

"McCrindle was an outstandingly good engineer, certainly one of the smartest people I have ever worked with though, ultimately, the relationship didn't work out."

Drummond Whiteford (another oilfield colleague) joined the business about a year after, in 1987. Another was Dick Rubbo. Then Drummond and Kinch and some others at PES later bought the McCrindle shareholding during 1991–93. Kinch describes it as a "messy process".

With all the chopping and changing, one issue for Kinch was how to keep his eye on the ball. He wanted to grow PES into an international force with a view to taking it public, whereas McCrindle had wanted it as a nice little cash earner – a hobby.

"We were making very good money and profitability was excellent. I had built a business as successful as anyone else I knew in the oil industry at that time in terms of turnover, size and profitability. Then I would look at the big service company names – Baker, Halliburton and others – and felt that what they were doing could be improved upon. They weren't technologically innovative whereas we were. They had to be pushed all the time. They were very conservative – like the oil majors.

"We generated a stream of good ideas and I could relate very closely to the oil companies because my background was both big service and major, so I could talk in the same 'language' as the petroleum engineers. I was looking for solutions, not just sell the tool but design a whole programme for delivering a solution."

How good is Kinch with people relationships as this is fundamental to success, not least for PES as it developed?

"I operate a very loose management structure. I don't believe in hierarchical structures. I like to surround myself with like-minded people and keep it relaxed. Inevitably, many of the people I employ are significantly sharper than I am – technically better than me. What I do is build a big picture and use people to colour it in. I think it must be there in me as I've never had formal management training.

"I'm often asked the question as to why I'm successful in business. Well, I've never run one without surrounding myself with talented people and I get them to buy into my vision. Two things drive people – the most important is intellectual challenge, the money is secondary. But the two are linked and you have to achieve both.

"In any company I have built, I see people during my day-to-day business who catch my attention. They're bright, aggressive, have great ideas and have much more potential outside the organisation they're working for. Inevitably I make contact with such guys and they join me. I'm very much a hands-off manager, which is why I take the title chairman. I step back and let my people get on with the day-to-day tasks."

So who were the people who really made PES happen, including the hallmark technology of the company, so-called "smart" well technology because of the ability to precision control flows from different zones within an oil reservoir?

"It was Dick and Drummond, plus Mike Bowyer (ex Baker Oil Tools) and Mike Fleming on day-to-day management. Mike Fleming didn't join until about 1994. I had spotted him at Scottish Enterprise. I initially took him on as commercial director but he went far beyond that."

By then, PES was probably approaching a turnover of £10–12 million and the smart well development work was almost a separate business. All the money was being generated by well intervention and completion products while the smart well development work was consuming most of it.

The business was divided into separate divisions covering the three core dis-ciplines: a major presence was grown in Aberdeen, another was established in Houston, and a manufacturing plant was set up near Edinburgh. In addition, regional offices were opened in France, Italy, Norway, Denmark. We were growing an empire.

Along the way, venture capital provider 3i took a £10 million stake in the company, an act that was to lead to another, totally different venture being set up; but the seminal deal was a bargain struck with US energy services giant Halliburton, which ultimately led to Kinch's creation being acquired.

Selling out – next step

In the Halliburton relationship, it was the US corporation that knocked on PES's door. It coincided with Kinch beginning to think that future growth was tied to developing a network of international sales and service outlets – an expensive, slow way forward.

"It wasn't what I wanted to invest in. I thought it much more appropriate for us to piggyback with a company that already had such a network. Halliburton stepped into the frame. The agreement struck was purely a franchise agreement where PES had access to that network."

Subsequently, they bought 26% of PES for £21 million in 1996. Kinch considered it an excellent fit, with the future of the pioneering smart well technology assured.

"It was only a matter of time before Halliburton would want to take total control, so I set myself the task of selling PES for £100 million. Up to that point, no one in Aberdeen had previously got anywhere near that sort of multiple.

"I'm glad to say I got £111 million in the end because I charged Halliburton interest as they were a bit slow in closing the deal; we finally closed in January 2000. It was a four-year process from taking the initial equity position to selling all PES."

Even before PES was a fully matured business, the Kinch mind was incubating the next idea. It was in 1993–94 when he saw what smart well could actually achieve – the value wasn't in building and selling such products, it was actually owning oil reservoirs and applying the smart technology to them.

Indeed, Kinch tried bouncing the idea off 3i at the time it was trying to buy a slice of PES.

"I recall a train journey to Edinburgh to watch a Scotland rugby game with Lawrence Ross and Keith Mair. They were trying to butter me up to buy into the business. I told them I had a better idea, I wanted to form an oil company. They said: 'Yes, yes, but we're here to talk about PES.'

"But I never stopped talking about my vision of setting up an independent exploration and production company.

"How that worked was that a friend who had been my line manager at BP when I was in Qatar – a guy called Dave Neely – he and I had talked about setting up a little independent oil company for quite a while and he was coming up for retirement.

"The then head of Energy at Scottish Enterprise, Hamish Dingwall, introduced me to his brother, Bruce, who had just bought some concessions in Trinidad. Bruce, Dave and I got together.

"The three of us set up a company called Venture Production with a £100,000 market capitalisation in 1996, each putting in £33,333. I later put a further £250,000 – they didn't have the cash and diluted their stakes. Later we took Mike Fleming into the company – he got 5% for £5,000 and I'm pleased to see that he made at least £1 million or more out of that."

That was the start of Venture, now a listed £400 million market cap UK oil company. But, around 1997–98 when trying to close off the Halliburton deal, Kinch became disconnected from Venture. At the same time, Neely decided he wanted to focus more on his retirement and a new relationship so he decided to opt out, leaving Bruce running the company. It is widely recognised that the last named later lost his way with the business.

Like PES, Kinch had seen Venture as a 'game-changer', which to some extent it has been. However, the company has not yet realised the original vision that he had way back when setting it up.

Making mistakes

"I think I made a mistake with Venture. I became too disconnected and the company lost focus. It didn't apply smart well technologies, even though it was sold on the mantra that technology would be key to its success."

Kinch justifies this by saying: "We found so much 'low hanging' fruit in the North Sea that we didn't need to apply smart technology."

As for management, Bruce Dingwall departed in 2004, leaving it to successor CEO Mike Wagstaff to get the business back on track which, by and large, he has.

"The company is producing north of 40,000 barrels of oil per day today and will grow output significantly near-term. I'm delighted with the way Venture is going today. Mike Wagstaff and his team have become much more focused and I think Venture will be using smart well and other cutting-edge technologies in the future."

What about his own position?

"I became re-engaged with Venture about two years ago and what really forced that was the Halliburton asbestos debacle in the US. I lost a fortune when Halliburton stock plummeted to next to nothing – about $8 compared with a high of $78. It cost me a lot of money.

"I realised then that it was difficult to make a fortune – but it's easy to lose it. I probably lost $30 million.

"I reflected on my life at that time. I had become complacent after the sale of PES. Then I found myself in 2000 with liquid assets north of $80 million – beyond my wildest dreams.

"At that point Venture was almost irrelevant to me. I did the playboy thing, apart from the women. I spent 2001 playing with my toys – high-performance cars. I was motor racing, shooting, I wasn't focused. Aside from the Halliburton thing and Venture's problems, the great thing is that I actually became bored with what I thought I wanted, which was to go and play with my racing cars. I was missing the corporate intellectual challenge. I remember waking up one day. It was a Venture board meeting. I said: 'Great, it's Venture board meeting today.' Then I checked myself and said: 'What!'

"I became engaged again. I had always attended the board meetings. I might not have been mentally there. Suddenly I switched back on. I detected that I had become a great concern for the likes of Bruce Dingwall. I didn't think the guy was performing.

"He had been drifting off. Maybe he was going through what I had been going through, only the difference was that he had a job to do; I'd already cashed out in one of my other companies. He did a great job between 1996 and 2000 – it was now time for a change."

This is an important part of the Kinch philosophy. He sees change as the only constant. There has to be constant reinvention or one dies. But he admits he cannot change himself.

"I'm always going to be as I am and that's one of the reasons why I don't put myself in a key position, such as CEO. Mine is an overview position. That's what stimulates me. But I still have enough time to do the other things I want to do in life. But the one thing I used to dream about – retiring in my 40s to go and play – I no longer want to do. Now I realise that I'll never retire.

"What I do is what I love best. Apart from my family, the thing I love most of all is my business. It's what gets me up in the morning. I enjoy it, I love it and I particularly love this new business – Energy Development Partners – because it's the culmination of all the things I've done to date – deal making, fiscal, technology, a talented team."

Strange new hybrid

Where did the idea for this rather strange hybrid come from? What triggered it?

"Ever since the point I sold PES and I was seen as a free agent, people were approaching me with business proposals and so forth. To be quite honest there was nothing that really turned my crank. I had done the service company, I'd done the E&P start-up, the major oil company career, I wanted to do something different.

"I looked at what I had achieved and looked at the roadblocks, which if they hadn't been there, would have allowed us to move much faster, and drew up a model of what I thought the company should look like and where it should fit.

"I had seen a lot of venture capitalists, for example, that put money into your business; they put cash in but they don't deliver anything thereafter. I said to myself that if they can raise money then surely I can raise money too but do something different."

In a nutshell, the idea was to create a company that can contribute funding to an oil company asset that is financially stranded, put in technical expertise, run that asset and take a slice of the production as the reward.

What differentiates it is that EDP is prepared to take 100% of the financial risk on a project and that, says Kinch, is really opening people's eyes.

Precedent? There is none that Kinch is aware of. He has searched for two years and, in the US, there is a fund called Quantum, but it is only partially similar. It would seem that the EDP model is unique and it comes from the combination of the skill sets Kinch has learned over the past 30 years. Moreover, he has experienced the financial side with raising money and taking Venture public, he has witnessed the poor uptake in the application of technology and he has seen the problems of going into auction rooms and trying to buy oil and gas assets.

"It was a case of let's come up with a solution. There's a problem out there. Auctions don't work because the person who wins the auction is probably the loser because he's probably overpaid; if it's a small company all the eggs are in one basket and all the capital has been used in buying it and exploration [for oil and gas] is like gambling. But I don't gamble.

"People on the outside may think I gamble. I don't. I believe I'm a very con-servative person. I only work in the areas I know. After 31 years in oil and gas business, I know this business. I can genuinely say I have a real feeling as to how trends and world markets and technology will evolve.

"Technology is actually the great provider for this industry, but many people fail to understand that. Without technology the industry would never have happened. I'm a huge believer in technology. It's like old Enzo Ferrari being asked the question: 'Which is the greatest car you've ever built?' He had one answer: 'My next one.'

"And I believe that with companies. I believe the EDP model is a development on what I've done in past years and it seems to be pretty successful. We have our first significant contract – it's with BP and we're about to close on our first fund – the first UK energy fund ever."

It all comes across as having happened almost instinctively. Indeed Kinch has never had formal business schooling.

"Maybe I have a natural talent. I'm described as an entrepreneur, but I don't feel that I am one. I've always worked within just this industry."

Has Lady Luck smiled?

"No, I've been unlucky compared to some. I know people who have set up businesses and one or two years on have sold out for huge sums of money, and they're often crap companies. Some fool walked through the door and paid them a huge premium."

6 RICHARD MARSH

TECHNO MOGUL

RICHARD MARSH

FACTFILE

Name	Richard John Marsh
Company	Tritech International Limited
Company turnover	£5 m
Current position	Managing Director
Place of birth	Cambridge, UK
Education	DTech, CEng, FIMech, FIEE
First job	Aircraft Design at British Aircraft Corporation
Best business decision	To leave a large company and start my own
Worst business decision	Not having done the above ten years earlier
Which company in the upstream oil and gas industry do you admire and why?	Apart from Tritech – one has to have a grudging admiration for the mergers and acquisitions which have created the current international market position that companies like Schlumberger and Fugro have achieved
Biggest dislike of the industry	Inability to present the right image of itself and its future to the great unwashed public and politicians. This has the sad consequence that we are failing to get the right message across to bright young engineers which makes it almost impossible to get them to join the industry
Advice to anyone considering a career in the oil industry	Ignore the propaganda and prejudice, you can have one of the most technically challenging and fulfilling careers possible in a thriving offshore oil industry that will continue until well after you retire
What do you think of management gurus?	I have been over exposed to them and have rarely been impressed. They generate endless patronising sound-bytes and management-speak cliches. You can boil every management textbook and presentation on the planet down to: focus, enthuse, never quit!
Favourite pastime	Caressing classic British cars back into life
Favourite book	*Oxford Book of English Verse*
Who or what is your inspiration?	The sublime engineering in a modern aircraft or a Formula 1 racing car inspires us to produce underwater equivalents. "The quality remains long after the price is forgotten" (Sir Henry Royce)
Any further ambitions?	Countless – I'm an old man in a hurry!
Favourite quote/saying	The greatest risk to business is not taking a risk

RICHARD MARSH

TECHNO MOGUL

Step into the unassuming offices of Tritech International, one of some 900 energy-related SMEs in and around Europe's energy capital, Aberdeen, and you will surely be surprised.

No, it won't be the huge toy tiger wearing shades that lounges across the back of the couch in reception. It might not even be a fine model of the tea clipper *Thermopylae* sitting on the boardroom table; or the stained-glass window depicting the world's first computer Colussus, which is a British World War II creation; or the fascinating bits of sonar and other underwater technologies that fill the laboratories and component assembly rooms; or a set of Concorde cockpit foot pedals.

Rather it is the managing director's office tucked in behind the reception desk – same size as everyone else's in the building, same level of décor and rarely with the door closed because Richard Marsh finds the trappings of corporate power anathema – not even a reserved space in the company car park.

That he is the one who collected two Queen's Awards for Enterprise, or the Royal Society of Edinburgh's Millennium Prize for SMEs, and various other awards, is neither here nor there. His view is that they are the result of a collective effort by a group of highly motivated people.

Marsh is passionate about technology. From Cambridge but with Scottish roots and a product of Central London Polytechnic – he has a degree in mechanical engineering – he was one of the team that designed and built Concorde at British Aerospace in Bristol.

At the project's zenith, he was responsible for the 1,600 highly skilled technicians and engineers who built the 16 Concordes completed in Britain. The young aeronautical engineer learned management skills relatively early, employing critical path analysis techniques to control the shop floor, and supervising quality standards.

But he detested the way in which senior management ran British Aerospace.

"I had joined British Aerospace as a right wing Tory pratt and one who thought that unions were the devil's creation because that's what I was told. After six months there I had total sympathy for trade unions," Marsh recalls.

"Over those 12 years, that company taught me everything I ever needed to know about how *not* to treat people.

"I decided that, if I ever set up my own company, I would do diametrically the opposite of every aspect of British Aerospace's behaviour and treatment of their staff.

"We joined as a bunch of graduate apprentices and, for reasons best known to management, I was promoted ahead of my peer group. It was the most miserable experience as the works engineers would come into my office and place a piece of carpet on the floor. One famous day, my pottery coffee mug was removed and replaced with bone china. Because I'd been promoted! Awful status distinction – symbols of position that I began to feel deeply uncomfortable about. Then I rose to the exalted level where I could pee in the director's lavatories, get free lunches and company cars.

"The organisation creating this wonderful aeroplane [Concorde] was riven with people playing internal politics for reasons of status and advance. I had joined as a fairly right wing character but, within four years, I had total sympathy for trade unions."

As the Concorde programme was running down in the mid-1970s, Marsh was given the opportunity to switch to underwater technology development, specifically remotely operated vehicles (ROVs). That the corporation was part-owned by Vickers has much to do with this.

Aviation to subsea

"There was obviously some sort of an exchange in the boardroom between directors, saying, we have all these bright young engineers that have just designed and built Concorde, why don't we create some unmanned submarines to save lives by replacing divers in the North Sea oil industry, which was getting underway at that time.

"I was given the job of working on the Consub project. This ROV was the size of a Ford Transit van with a 50bhp power unit. It was designed by Concorde engineers and was the most amazing remotely operated vehicle on planet Earth. We built ideas into Consub 30 years ago that aren't yet in modern ROVs.

"In 1977 I brought Consub to Aberdeen to try and sell it and was laughed out of town by companies like BP.

"In the same way as it was then thought that the world market for computers was five systems, I was told by BP that there was a world market for one ROV. I was told to go away. 'We're always going to use divers, you'll never replace man's hands,' they said. 'We can do nothing with ROVs.'

"I remember very depressing sleepless nights. I'd given up my aerospace job, I'd left my wife and family in Bristol and here I was in Aberdeen trying to flog ROVs.

"In fact I realised Consub was economic nonsense as soon as I got up to Aberdeen and tried to sell the thing for £800,000, which was a serious amount of money when the Americans were selling systems for £200,000. Even I could work out that the factor of four was quite a disadvantage.

Consub had to be cancelled; it was economic nonsense. However, I knew ROVs had a future because God didn't invent divers to go underwater. I was convinced there was a serious market for the right type of vehicles and control systems, but nobody would believe me."

In the end, Marsh went out and tried to do it for himself and, on 1 January 1979, with Norwegian capital because he had no money of his own, he started a company called Bennico down by Aberdeen Harbour.

The reason why the oil companies weren't interested in ROVs at that time was because all the major diving companies then, and sometimes with oil company support, were building support ships with 16-man, 24-man, even 28-man saturation diving systems on board.

"The last thing they were going to do was listen to an idiot little Englishman who claimed that they didn't need all that and could replace it with a robot that could do most of the work. I was told to bugger off – it's nonsense – rubbish.

"I was getting nowhere. My company was rapidly heading for bust. The Norwegians were hassling me, saying I had £10,000 of their money for which they were getting zero return."

Then Marsh had a brilliance. He changed tack and, instead of pushing the tech-nology *per se*, started to examine the econometrics of ROVs versus divers. Even in those days, it could cost £50,000 to examine 100 metres of pipeline using divers.

"When I started down the econometrics route the companies had to listen. What I had started to do was offer a solution – not just a technology. There I was, a naïve engineer spouting on about high tech that would so blindingly obviously save money, but until I quantified just how much, they were going to keep saying, 'Buzz off silly little man – go home.'

"They had to start paying attention, particularly drilling rig support people. Rigs didn't need divers, all they needed was one low-cost ROV hanging off a fishing vessel for a few quid a day. It could do the whole job.

"Finally, we began to percolate through the industry. It was like a tsunami with the sea going out for a year then, whoosh, it became a headlong rush and suddenly we were selling ROVs like crazy.

Riding a tiger

"One day, sitting in the Yardarm Bar at Aberdeen Harbour – I treated it like an extension to my office – I clearly remember having lunch and I felt like a VIP compared with being totally rejected six months before.

"There would be a bunch of people from Oceaneering waiting to talk to me, a bunch from Seaway Diving, another from Subsea – all wanting to buy ROVs from me. It was amazing. It was one long party and we sold loads. There were 1,500 saturation divers in the North Sea then, but that population plummeted rapidly from then on. I don't know how many are left."

However, Marsh was to get tired of filling Norwegian pockets through his efforts. Very little of Bennico's turnover was being pumped into the local economy. He was also fed up with seeing intellectual property flowing out of Britain to Norway and the US, so he determined to change that, create British subsea products and export them, and the lynchpin technology would be sonar systems for oil industry, survey and military applications.

"So, in a low-key way one winter I started Tritech – a 100% British/Scottish company starting with modest little products that I was able to afford.

"I loved the idea of starting the company. Besides the technology, only by running my own firm could I actually establish the culture and ideas I had for managing people. Starting Tritech was stimulating – fun – fraught. But I like stress – fraught is fun for me to some extent. I'm a bit of a sad case in that regard. I get into awful mischief if I get bored; I have to create stress."

One issue faced by many budding entrepreneurs with wife or partner is how to broach the subject. And the Marsh way?

"I think she was told rather than asked. I made some very false promises to her that we had enough money after Bennico so as not to have to do very much because, by this time, the children's education was more or less complete. They were at decent schools and universities, we had a big house in the country – we could always sell that – I misled her. I said I was going to make this a sort of easy job. In reality I started and continue to ride a tiger.

"From time to time she reminds me that Tritech was meant to be me running down. It's ridiculous, I'm 61 for goodness' sake. But I'm more motivated, more enthusiastic and more ambitious (but not for myself) than ever before.

"It's very interesting and I wouldn't have believed this in the past. Making money is probably eighth or tenth on the list of things that make me happy. I've no more interest in making money.

"I'm driven by the desire to create super-high technology productions, to get the satisfaction of the Brazilians using them, the Singaporeans using them and beating the French at it; oh, and seeing NATO neighbours with Tritech sonars on their submarines.

Not for the money

"I don't really care if nobody pays me a penny for any of that. The fact that we've done it, that we've achieved it, that we've beaten our competitors at their own game and shown that Britain still can produce world-class products and beat anybody, gives me far more satisfaction than whether you pay me a pound or a million pounds. But then I'm comfortable. I don't need money."

That said, he confesses to deriving great satisfaction in seeing the company making profits for without profits the dream would be harder to realise. The particular global market that Tritech addresses is worth only £10 million or so, and yet this modest SME has most of it.

Behind the almost mad professor exterior is a razor sharp mind at work. Marsh's obsession is about translating his love of technology into delivering solutions. Underpinning that are various methodologies and techniques for coming up with ideas that are going to sell.

"You have to analyse anything you take from concept to money in the bank – there are a lot of rigorous processes going on. It needs to be robust, it needs determination, inspiration, leadership and, above all else, it needs enthusiasm.

"There are various things that you must bring to the table to get from a silly idea to money in the bank, which is what this business is all about. That's what I love. It makes you a very broad human being because you have to handle so much – not just technology but human beings (who can be most unpredict-able).

"You have to be determined about things. You've got to know when you're wrong, when you're right – you've got to keep going when all around you would give up. And somehow, if you have a sense of humour, you can summarise all of that as fun.

"All those experiences – even the most negative – can in one sense be fun in that you learn from them and you're going to have a better life in the future. You sometimes cynically say it's fun when reality is far from it."

Marsh admits that he needs strong people in the Tritech business that are capable of standing up to him.

"There is a tendency when you're running a small company to bully people unwittingly," he confesses. "You just get enthusiastic. What you don't realise is that your people are constantly aware of the fact that you pay them and you can sack them and they sort of have to go along.

"I hate the ownership of power in one sense because it does destroy relationships."

One way in which Marsh deals with this dilemma is to have one-to-one conversations, aka personal development reviews.

"In some ways you have to be a psychologist. You have to look after your people. Ask them what the most important thing is and the replies are profit, customer satisfaction – that sort of thing. Tell them the most important thing in the company is recruitment – it's about people.

"You have to make sure you have a one-to-one relationship with all your staff, that they're not being intimidated by you – the best trick I can play on that one with people is ask them what they think. You help me – you tell me, I haven't a clue.'

"Often I'll already know the answer – sounds arrogant – and I keep my fingers crossed under the table. They come up with the idea, I say 'good, go and do it'. I'm probably wondering what it's going to cost the company, but I have to give them their head – you have to develop people."

Marsh claims that when handling staff that his instinct tells him are stronger than he is, he has never felt threatened in that business sense and that's a source of regret to him.

Take my job ... please

"It's a pity. I'd love somebody to take my job so I can wind down a bit. I'd love to have someone to develop and grow but I haven't found anyone yet.

"I want people to be stronger than I am. I'm recruiting the very best people I can't afford. Who was it who said you should have five or six people in your team who can do a better job than you and that you then pay them more than you pay yourself?

"Indeed, there are five or six people in this company to whom I pay more than I pay myself. That's important, but then I own 80% of the company."

This is also Marsh's oblique way of trying to solve the succession issue at Tritech as he has no family in the business. Those five or six are hired to develop the company and, if out of that emerges a future leader, then he says it would be "beneficial serendipity".

"I haven't gone out to directly recruit successors at all; I've gone out to recruit people who can do a good job. I don't care whether I'm 61 or 31; age is irrelevant to me unless I suddenly have a heart attack. I should be planning succession."

There is a very vulnerable side to this much lauded businessman – he gets to "like and love" the people he works with and gets terribly upset if there is an abuse of trust. This happened in 2005 when it proved necessary to sack two people for low-grade fraud. They had betrayed Marsh's trust.

So what does the future really hold for this remarkable individual?

"I'm still creative – maybe more than ever before. I don't think I've lost too many brain cells through drinking three distilleries in my life. I don't know about the brain cells, but I have a weight of experience and knowledge and feel for what products are needed.

"I'm just doing a job. I'm very privileged to create the toys I like to create. It's lovely. I feel a sense of privilege all the time. Generally speaking, this is a very happy company. I love it.

"One of my standing jokes at home is that I am fully retired. I'm doing exactly what I want to do. If retirement means painting the blinking kitchen or playing an idiotic game of golf you can keep it.

"This is retirement. This is defining how I want to live. It's far more fun than anything I've ever seen in retirement. I'm fully retired now."

Message to students

"I love seeing young people start companies – I love encouraging them. That's why I'm helping at Aberdeen Business School and mentoring, also sitting on the Royal Society of Edinburgh Fellowship.

"I get very envious of Philip Green and the *Sunday Times* rich list but then I check myself and remind myself that I've done what I want – played with technology.

"I've shown, not that I can beat the world at trading in ladies shoes or underwear, Pizza Express or Vodafone, but that my team can beat the world in technological niches where there has been serious high technology competition and yet we've won. Future generations can do the same thing, if they have a mind to."

8 ARTHUR MILLHOLLAND

INDEPENDENT MOGUL

ARTHUR MILLHOLLAND

FACT FILE

Name	Arthur Millholland
Company	Oilexco Incorporated
Company turnover	Stated oil and gas revenues CAD$2.7 million
Current position	President and CEO
Place of birth	Ontario, Canada
Education	BSc (Hons) Earth Sciences, University of Waterloo, Waterloo, Ontario
First job	Exploration Geologist, Sulpetro Limited
Best business decision	To change the focus of Oilexco to the North Sea
Worst business decision	To spend time pursuing opportunities in the Middle East
Which company in the upstream oil and gas industry do you admire and why?	I admire several past and present North American independent oil companies, especially those run by characters
Biggest dislike of the industry	Short sightedness
Advice to anyone considering a career in the oil industry?	Good things will come to you, if you have patience
What do you think of management gurus?	They should be relegated to the dustbin
Favourite pastime	Road racing my car
Favourite book	Chuck Yeager's Biography
Who or what is your inspiration?	Declined to answer
Any further ambitions?	Declined to answer
Favourite quote/saying	Declined to answer

ARTHUR MILLHOLLAND

INDEPENDENT MOGUL

Arthur Millholland is a big man. He is the president of Oilexco, a small Canadian oil "independent" that in 2004 and 2005 stormed into North Sea headlines because of its bold exploits with Brenda, an oil discovery made in 2004 by the company and which could yield tens of millions of barrels of oil, once developed.

Small, so-called exploration and production companies like this are where much of the future of the UK North Sea lies – compact, nimble and apparently better at making money out of existing but tired oil and gas fields and opening up new, small accumulations deemed uneconomic by oil majors like BP and Shell.

It is the Oilexcos of this world that the North Sea oil and gas supply chain is now having to come to terms with and invent new ways of business that complement the strategic goals of such companies. They are diverse and growing in number, with a host of different business models applied, of which only some will ultimately succeed.

But what makes Millholland think he can make it in this high-cost energy province, especially given his background – the onshore oil and gas industry of Canada where the game is totally different? And that's the point. It is because the game is so totally different in Canada than the North Sea, because small companies have been so adept at dealing with insignificant fields in difficult locations, that Millholland is convinced that they are what is needed to get the best out of Britain's remaining offshore reserves, which are currently calculated to be roughly in the range 20–30 billion barrels oil equivalent.

"The first thing people have to understand is that we have 3,500 oil companies in Canada today," says Millholland. "Twenty-five years ago it was dominated by the 'Seven Sisters', big multi-nationals like BP, Shell and Texaco. But then they decided that all of the oil had effectively been found and so they pulled out, leaving an air of doom and gloom in Calgary; much the same sort of thing that has been happening in the North Sea during the past number of years. What we found in Canada was that, though the remaining opportunities for the big guys were limited, the picture was completely different when you looked at it from the perspective of the small company.

"We Canadians are hands-on people and I'm a petroleum geologist by trade. All of the managers are technical people and everyone lives the business. And the business in Canada is extremely competitive because of the number of players – probably the most competitive in the world. But the opportunities there are now getting smaller which means the level of risk is increasing."

Recognising this risk, Millholland started casting around for alternative opportunities about a decade ago and one of the first places he looked at outwith North America was the UK. That was in 1996.

"We felt at that time that there were lots of reasons to be here, but the opportunities were poor because the original licences [to exploit North Sea resources] were in the early days given out [to mostly large oil companies] on overly favourable terms and there were issues to do with this. One result was that the cost of entry in 1996 was too high for us. Things had to change before we could try again.

Cost of entry too high

"When we came back and looked at it in 2001, because of actions by the UK Department of Trade & Industry with regard to North Sea acreage lying idle, we felt the time was right – that there were opportunities for people such as ourselves."

But Millholland, who now has an AIM-listed UK subsidiary based out of Aberdeen, is not interested in cast-off oil and gas fields that are on their last legs economically. To him that is buying the prior incumbent's problems. His focus is on promising geology that might harbour yet to be discovered resources and on unexploited discoveries that should prove economic if the right development approach is applied.

"We're not talking about wild and crazy exploration. We're really focused on undeveloped discoveries and wells that tested oil, using our strength, which is seismic data reprocessing. We've devoted a great deal of effort to that."

But that's the easy bit. More difficult is raising enough money to be able to deliver commercial development capable of washing its face economically.

"We have to finance that on the basis that you cannot go out there and raise money blindly; well I guess you can with oil prices how they are right now, around $50 per barrel, as there's some silly money in the City. With a set programme, we can go to the financial markets in Canada and in the UK and seek the funding we need."

In June 2005 Oilexco announced that it was seeking to raise up to £30.4 million in an offering of new shares to fund its ongoing programme and that the shares would be offered in the Canadian provinces of Alberta, British Columbia and Ontario, but primarily in the UK.

Earlier, in April 2004, the company successfully closed a US$38 million special warrant offering to investors outside of Canada. Then, in February 2005, it raised some £7 million before expenses through a private placing of 5.385 million new shares with European institutions and, in May, it signed a £10 million bridging loan facility with Royal Bank of Scotland that will enable the ordering of certain long lead-time items for the intended development of the Brenda oil discovery.

There is little doubt that Millholland has been successful in his efforts and most of the money has been found in Britain, which is contrary to the commonly held UK domestic belief that it is easier for junior oil companies to find backing in North America – Canada and the US.

"You know, there's a new generation of fund managers in London and our timing is right. We attracted attention when we said we're going to operate our oil and gas assets. We're not going to sit back and be a passive partner, we're going to control our destiny.

"But, when we came up with a business plan that said we were going to operate – control our own destiny, the fact is that we had never operated an offshore well before. I said to my team that, once one gets below the seabed, it's no different to drilling on land. We can hire the expertise to get us out there into the North Sea and below the seabed.

"So when we came to Aberdeen, we hired Peak Well Management as our well engineering partner. We went to the DTI where we stood up and admitted we have never drilled offshore but that we could do it in a safe and efficient manner, and low-cost, and here's how we're going to do it."

Most of this happened in 2002 at a time when Oilexco's domestic turnover was just over $1.5 million Canadian. It was much the same the following year too. In financial terms, progress had been slow since the company was established in 1993.

Taking control of own destiny

Millholland had set up Oilexco on the basis that he had spent long enough working for others – the first company was Solpetrol, but the time had come to take direct control of his destiny. A geology graduate of University of Waterloo in Eastern Canada, he managed to secure backing and set out to seek his fortune. It sounds hackneyed, but that's how it was.

"I was young, I figured I could do as well as anybody else, so I quit my job and went to work for myself. I thought it would be easy, but it wasn't.

"Oilexco was set up to do exploration – that was what the shareholders wanted. But that's a high-risk game. You can drill nothing but dry holes and we drilled an awful lot of those."

However, Millholland is convinced that he is getting it right in the North Sea and that the Brenda exploration success is clear evidence of that. Moreover, he reckons there are many more, similar accumulations in the North Sea.

"Where we come from in Canada, this type of accumulation is more the norm than the exception. We understand them a lot better than people here do. When we came into the business it was routine; for us, things that we take as second nature in terms of the steps we take to evaluate. But this leads to conflict here because people here aren't used to it.

"So we're in the process of getting to that point. We've hired staff, the Brenda development plan is almost ready for filing with the DTI and we're moving towards getting it on production within a year (some time in 2006).

"We think that's about as fast as it's ever been done. Again, it's a mind set – rather than say we can't do something, we prefer to believe we can do anything we want. It's about having the right people – doing something simple and getting it done."

But how has it been for a can-do Canadian to come into a climate where people will still think of reasons why not to do something, rather than grasping the bull by the horns?

"We've been lucky. We've found some very good people here; we've met them over the past three years. They're people with a light shining from within. Some really talented people have even come and asked whether they can join us.

"We're grafters. We're after people with a special skill-set. We're not after people who are afraid to make recommendations though, at the end of the day, I'm the one who says yes or no. But, at the same time, people do drill dry holes – that's a fact of life. We've been very lucky here so far."

What will ultimately make the difference for Millholland and his team is the way in which they engage with the UK North Sea supply chain – with people like those highlighted in this book. It will require flair and imagination and not a little forwardness. And Oilexco's president has that aplenty as demonstrated by the contract struck with Peak Well Services regarding management of the drilling programme, but more particularly the way in which he set about hiring a rig to drill those wells. Millholland did what many in the North Sea community instantly judged foolhardy, stupid even – he hired a semi-submersible drilling rig not just for a few wells but for two whole years.

Shrewd drilling deal

Pundits said this was the sort of thing that big oil companies did, not thinly resourced minnows.

"The most important thing when you're embarking on something like we're doing is to look at the tools you need to hire and decide on the best way to secure them and for how long. With Brenda, last year we looked at the rig market – it was getting tighter and rates were rising; we looked at oil prices and they were headed north for a time at least. We decided that, having found Brenda, we'd better get it fully developed and on production as soon as we could.

"I foresaw that the rig market would tighten up and capacity would disappear. So we started talking to fleet owner Transocean in July 2004 about a rig for 2005. We signed an agreement in September for the rig Sedco 712 – a year's contract from March '05 to March '06 with the option of taking it on for a further one year.

"Then I did something that's never really been done before as we really only had three months' worth of work for the rig. I said, 'We have nine months to put this drilling rig to work. Let's go find some more opportunities that we can drill, using that rig as leverage.'"

By that, Millholland means securing additional North Sea acreage by bargaining Oilexco's way into a stake and saying that it already had a rig standing by to get drilling, subject to satisfactory data on target prospects.

"What we've been able to say is that we have the rig and we've rolled over our service contracts. In the last year we started off being prepared to drill two wells – and we've ended up being the most active operator in the UK sector. And we'd just started out from scratch."

Millholland says Oilexco's entry into the North Sea is perfectly timed with no shortage of opportunities and that, in two to three years' time (2007–08), he intends to be at the head of a "significant" company. Among steps taken include buying into established oil production via stakes in the Balmoral and Glamis fields secured in September 2004.

Every step taken in the North Sea is made all the easier because the UK still has about the best fiscal terms in the world, something that Millholland is keen to highlight.

"It's transparent – there's no corruption here, unlike many other countries in the world. And a contract's a contract. People speak the same language. It sounds prejudiced but, for Canadians, working in the UK is like working at home. Same language, too, and ancestors in common."

The goal is laudable, but what makes this geologist with zero management training so certain?

"I'll have to delegate more responsibility," is the reply. "I can't do everything. We're hiring good people and we trust them.

"I work entirely instinctively; I've never been to management school. At the end of the day, I'm here to make money. My background is working for oil and gas independents; I've never worked for a large company."

But he has had mentors, people who have been willing to give of their time to help the young oil entrepreneur and the first was called Gus van Mielingen. "He was what you would call one of the last old-time North American oilmen – what people called a wildcatter. He was a gambler. That was way back. The business these days is primarily run by accountants and one of the results of where we are today as an industry, and really amplified in the North Sea, is that the oil majors are trying to remove all the risks to the business. But you cannot do that in upstream oil and gas and that's why so little has been happening in the North Sea, because of that mindset, that culture where risk has to be eliminated."

From risk to common decency

"There are exploration and appraisal departments in some companies where, if you drill a dry hole, you get fired. I tend to look at it and say, well, you learn from them. Sure they're expensive learning experiences [a single North Sea well can cost millions of dollars to drill] but, at the same time, if you have a team that has confidence in themselves, how you nurture that confidence is to say: 'OK it was a dry hole, now let's pick ourselves up and move on to the next one.'

"Truthfully, what we're doing here in the North Sea isn't that risky. We believe there's a reward. Of course, the Brenda accumulation may not be as large as we think it is – or it could be larger.

"Reality is that you cannot take all risk out of the equation. The inactivity here in the North Sea spells madness. In the past they've [oil companies] been saying: 'We know there's oil there in that field [Brenda], but is it 10 million barrels or is it 50 million? Because there is the risk that it may be 10 million, that doesn't fit our criteria, so we're not going to do anything about it.'

"Our view is that it's 50:50 – now let's work out why. Look at the finds statistically, and everything here in the North Sea has been under-estimated. The opportunities here are very economic to pursue, even on low case. That's what makes us very excited. And that's what I've got from all these other people in the past.

"If you can stomach the risk and have the guts then you can make a fortune in this business."

But attempting to make a fortune is not the be all and end all for Millholland; that is very evident from a side of his life that in 2000 earned him the Canadian YMCA Peace Medal. Canadians feel very strongly about the impact of conflict on the mothers and children of Iraq. He finds the whole affair repugnant.

"I went to Iraq and was appalled at what I saw. The West has got rid of Saddam Hussein, but you don't do that sort of thing at the cost of the mothers and children of that country."

Millholland made 25 trips over three years, engaging in shuttle diplomacy and being involved in the United Nations oil for food programme, including organising two cargoes of crude in exchange for food and medicines, while side-stepping the associated bribes payments scandal that enveloped others. He was also involved in pressuring the Canadian government to remove the economic sanctions that had been hurting ordinary Iraqis so badly, while leaving in place the military sanctions.

Millholland was nominated for the YMCA Peace Medal by Donn Lovett, vice-president/prairies of the United Nations Association in Canada, and Edmund A. Oliverio, director of the Alberta Centre for Ethics.

Awarding the citation on 15 November 2000, Oliviero said: "Mr. Millholland is an example to the oilpatch and to the business community that corporations that exercise corporate responsibility can make a difference to promote the principles of a culture of peace in our community and in our world."

If this is a measure of the man, then Arthur Millholland should make his mark on the North Sea too.

9 JIMMY MILNE

PERSISTENT MOGUL

JIMMY MILNE

FACTFILE

Name	James Smith Milne
Company	Balmoral Group Ltd
Company turnover	2003: £51 m
Current position	Chairman and Managing Director
Place of birth	Aberdeen
Education	Torry Academy and the University of Life.
First job	Agricultural Engineer
Best business decision	The creation of Balmoral Park as the global headquarters for Balmoral Group Ltd
Worst business decision	Not appreciating the value of good advice and business mentors during the early days
Which company in the upstream oil and gas industry do you admire and why?	Wood Group. From humble beginnings in Aberdeen a truly global player has emerged under the inspirational leadership of Sir Ian Wood
Biggest dislike of the industry	The imbalance that exists between multi-national operating companies, contractors and suppliers
Advice to anyone considering a career in the oil industry?	The energy industry is a dynamic and innovative environment in which to forge a career. Novel and positive thinkers, and those not afraid to rock the boat, will excel
What do you think of management gurus?	Wait a moment 'til I ask my management guru!
Favourite pastime	Spending time with my family
Favourite book	The Bible
Who or what is your inspiration?	My family and colleagues
Any further ambitions?	To position Balmoral at the peak of each of its chosen operating sectors
Favourite quote/saying	Never say "I can't achieve that"; always ask, "How can I achieve that"

JIMMY MILNE

PERSISTENT MOGUL

In September 1999, Balmoral Group of Aberdeen secured a $55 million contract for deepwater buoyancy systems with French oil major Total that came close to being the undoing of the Aberdeen company. So much money was ploughed into research and development associated with the technology that it led to a forced merger of its oil-related business with the company's prime competitor in order to survive.

But battling against adversity is nothing new to Balmoral's founder/ chairman, Jimmy Milne, who in May 2005 celebrated the 25th anniversary of the company with a celebratory dinner at Balmoral Castle. Milne, now in his mid-sixties, stated his determination to stick around for many years to come and well he might for this physically fit son of an Aberdeenshire farmer is among the most dogged entrepreneurs to come out of northeast Scotland and, unlike the other moguls profiled in this book, he has lived through a company collapse.

Arguably, Milne is also more of a showman than the others, as illustrated by a crazy stunt he pulled off in August 1998, at the time of the Offshore Northern Seas oil show in Stavanger. He quite literally dropped in on an island garden party being staged by the Norwegian arm of the group. He had only once before used a parachute, practising just the previous day for the drop. He pulled it off – a calculated risk that worked. As much as anything else, it was to tell Balmoral staff and oil industry guests at the time that he was firmly in control of the business.

This boldness coupled with dogged determination has much if not everything to do with the way he was brought up on a farm, just to the south of Aberdeen and not far at all from the headquarters of Balmoral Group at Loirston. Indeed his birthplace, Home Farm, has been not far from everything significant tackled by this robust, globetrotting Scot.

"Ever since I was a wee kid I always knew that one day I'd be on my own," says Milne, casting his mind back to those days. "I didn't know where, what or when and I didn't tell anybody." There was no question about it, I just knew that one day I'd be on my own. Simple as that."

That was in the late 1940s when Britain was struggling to recover after six years of war.

Milne, the youngest of nine siblings, did not want to be trapped on the land, where all had learned to pull their weight from a very early age. His was a love–hate relationship with his father.

"I used to be not too happy about my Dad, I can tell you. He had to be dead and gone before I appreciated him. He died in an accident in 1966. I found him.

"My brothers worked on the farm, but I made my mind up at an early age that I wasn't going to stay."

Like everyone else in this book, Milne also wanted to be an engineer. That way, if agriculture was to be his lot then at least he would be well equipped as this most traditional of industries embraced mechanisation. And like about half the individuals profiled in this book, Milne left school early. He was a self-confessed disaster, except for technical subjects; he could not wait to escape once aged 14.

"I was always 27th out of 29 in the class! I'm not proud of that. But in things I liked – metalwork, woodwork – I was top."

Milne might have hated farm life, but he was fast to latch onto business oppor-tunities when in his teens – like mushroom growing and hiring cars. That ignited a fire of entrepreneurship that has burned brightly ever since, through thick and thin.

The teenager was then serving his time with agricultural engineering firm Barclay, Ross and Hutcheson, ultimately spending 10 years with the company – welding, turning, fitting and mechanics.

Grasping the nettle

Around 1963, while reflecting on the massive levels of corrosion that muck spreading and other agricultural equipment was prone to, Milne felt there had to be a way around the problem as, short of galvanising everything, paint systems of the day gave only short-term protection.

This led to the question, why not manufacture some components using fibreglass, then a new technology, rather than steel? There again, why not cut loose from Barclay, Ross and Hutcheson and exploit the technology? In any case, Milne felt exploited by his employer and it finally came to a head.

"I went to my boss and asked for a pay increase. But he said: 'You're not getting one.' I said: 'Fine Jim, I'll just leave.' I needed someone to kick me out because I loved my job. He said I wasn't worth more money."

Thus Milne was cast out onto the entrepreneurship road! He determined to pursue the fibreglass idea and was to devote three years to researching the then wonder technology. Basically, Milne was embracing the plastics revolution while keeping himself afloat financially by growing mushrooms, lettuces, hiring cars or whatever.

"In business you've to be a good wheeler-dealer, you have to have business acumen, you have to be streetwise, have ambition, and have stamina. I used to work mad hours, up to eleven o'clock, midnight, then I'd be up again at 4am."

Milne hatched a plan to build a factory at Stonehaven, 15 miles south of Aberdeen, to make fibreglass products. Planning permission was sought and gained, the land was organised, but his bank refused to play ball by lending money.

"As far as they were concerned, I was too young and I'd never proved myself in business."

So Milne turned to Plan B, the mushroom shed at Home Farm. This ex-RAF building that had originally cost £20 was cleaned up and turned into a fibreglass moulding facility. It was the cheap option and just as well as there were few customers – nearby and established competitor Mouldacraft had the market.

However, further north in Fraserburgh was CPT, a firm that had been involved none too successfully in developing a glass fibre shell cover for road compressors. Milne said he would solve the troubles and make a shell at no cost to prove it. Six months went into designing and making a prototype, by which time CPT had reverted to steel fabrication. It was a blow at the time, but Milne at least had a demonstrator piece to market to potential clients: "I still think it was one of the best pieces we ever made – a work of art."

Indeed that prototype compressor cover was to launch Milne's first proper business, Northeast GlassFibre Works Ltd, which later evolved into Aberglen Group. Not content with organic growth alone, Milne attempted to buy Mouldacraft from owner Sparks for £40,000 and set a 24-hour deadline for a response. The offer was thrown out – Sparks wanted around £100,000. But Milne persisted, won the day and then went out to raise the money – all £40,000! Fortunately the bank was willing this time.

"I paid that loan off in six months flat."

The transition to Aberglen was rapid but, by 1974, growth was under threat because Aberdeen had become a klondike town, awash with oil money. Milne needed more space but building costs had gone through the roof, so the decision was taken to hire a construction team directly and self-build.

The net result was that Aberglen got the space it needed, plus a new division was added to the company – Aberglen Construction – an enterprise that was to become the biggest municipal builder in Aberdeen at the time. What it demonstrated at the time was that either Milne was plain lucky or he genuinely had the business knack.

Certainly the mid-1970s anecdote around Aberdeen was that he had the Midas touch. This was a reflection of the fact that Aberglen had also internationalised into more than 20 markets, before refining that side of the business down to basically Iran and Nigeria, because they generated the best returns.

Losing the Midas touch

But then Milne lost his golden touch. At the end of 1979, the Iran market nose-dived. Eight weeks later, Nigeria went the same way. Instead of pulling out, Milne hung in and by doing so made a huge tactical mistake.

"My success became my failure. I was so buoyed up with confidence I thought I could change the world. I felt I was king. Wrong! Wrong! Wrong!"

The bankers to Aberglen, then employing about 1,000, stepped in to assist. Millions of pounds were loaned. At the same time, interest rates rocketed and debts were mounting. Then the Inland Revenue demanded some £250,000 in unpaid PAYE and Aberglen was required to settle or else be liquidated. For Milne, that was the final straw. He had only one way out and that was to call in the receivers. This decision was apparently made against bank advice and the deed was done on 14 March 1980.

"I saw a wee light at the end of the tunnel and I was so fast through that tunnel it was unreal."

Milne now looks back on that episode with the benefit of hindsight and experience. He says a more considered approach would now be taken, including taking appropriate advice.

At the time, Aberglen's collapse was major news in the northeast of Scotland. Milne had committed a cardinal sin – he owed money and on his home patch. And he was in the headlines again six months later when it emerged that he was setting up in business again, an action that rankles with some former creditors even today, because Milne had the temerity to bounce back.

"In September 1980, I started up again. I didn't want to. It was morally wrong to me. But I was under pressure from customers, from employees and fed up with the receiver who failed to sell Aberglen."

He says it was a newspaper headline that made him launch out again in Aberdeen, this time choosing the name Balmoral for a firm that would initially design and manufacture fibreglass products such as storage tanks, navigation aids and modular buildings. Defending the decision, he says a lot of creditors were paid ultimately.

"I had the same bank, the same suppliers, the same customers and I got terrific help from them. I emerged from that a somewhat wiser person and very much more mature with feet planted more firmly on the ground. I had spent six months sitting at home. I was devastated. I had let a lot of people down. Even today, some people still hold it against me. But, if you're sensible, you learn huge lessons.

"As a result, building Balmoral into a diverse group has been a somewhat slower, more deliberate process than the halcyon days of Aberglen. Teamwork from the shop floor to the boardroom is considered core to the group's success."

Whether Balmoral's growth has been more considered is a moot point as Milne has always nursed high ambition, and why not. It is a trait that should be admired and not criticised. The problem in his case is that there are those who would wish him to crash and burn.

For sure, Milne has attempted to do some things with Balmoral that have failed to reach their full potential, and that includes full development of the sprawling site that the company occupies at Loirston. And, while it is fair to say that he has an astonishingly loyal top team and workforce, perceptually the rift some years ago between himself and much younger brother-in-law, Mark Patterson, was not helpful. Mark had been MD for some while prior to the split, which made local headlines at the time.

For its size, Balmoral is among the heaviest investors in pushing back the frontiers of technology in Britain; witness the huge commitment made to developing buoyancy modules for the Girassol project offshore West Africa. From the earliest dabbling in fibreglass, it is fair to say that this company is responsible for some of the most advanced plastics technologies in Europe today.

Total hell

The Total work had been bid in 1998 and secured in September 1999 against fierce competition from a narrow field of companies specialising in syntactic foam technologies that would be used to manufacture a huge number of insulating buoyancy modules for clamping around sophisticated pipework linking seafloor wellheads with a giant oil production ship that the French energy company was having built for its Girassol development offshore Nigeria.

Milne tabled his bid on the back of prior experience manufacturing similar modules for deepwater drilling rigs, but this job was different, very different.

"It turned into a roller-coaster. They [Total] changed the specification slightly which meant we had to change the chemistry of our syntactic foam process."

Basically, Balmoral had to change the technology and it was a task that proved a nightmare, even though the group had the most advanced plant in the world for the manufacture of syntactic foam products.

"The plant was years ahead of the competition and yet it wasn't good enough to deal with a Girassol type mix. It meant major modifications and, quite frankly, it was the most difficult thing we have ever tackled. The Girassol buoyancy modules were for the deepest oilfield development ever attempted offshore West Africa. The contract was for $55 million and Balmoral spent $20 million on R&D, with thousands of modules manufactured before the syntactic recipe was deemed correct for the task.

"It burnt up a number of Balmoral staff but, give the guys their due, they worked 14, 16, even 18 hours a day week in, week out for months on end. And in the end they produced the product within time. They get 10 out of 10 for what was an incredible effort."

The sad thing about $2 billion Girassol is that Total could see Balmoral was hurting badly and failed to take action. Is Milne bitter? He claims not but the following words suggest otherwise.

"Without those buoyancy modules, Girassol would not be delivering oil today if it wasn't for Balmoral, and we're a small company. We did not get the compensation we should have done. They promised, but we didn't get it and that's bad.

"The oil industry has to waken up quite frankly. Only a few short years ago they used to pay companies in the supply chain to carry out R&D for future projects. Now they throw it onto you and you're expected to do it, and they're the ones making all the profits. I think their behaviour is totally unfair. They're making billions of pounds in profits right now with oil at $50 a barrel. They had our support a few years ago when oil was down below $10; indeed Balmoral was one of the first companies to respond when they tried to drive costs down.

"Why did I accept? Because it helped drive technology and sharpened the mind, but the problem was they got it too easily. Then they wanted another 20%, but they weren't happy with that, and then they wanted further cuts as oil prices climbed back past $20 a barrel.

"They need innovative contractors like us. Of course I like to do things bigger and better than everyone else or at least try. But it's at great cost and I don't think we're valued enough. There are no hard feelings. I'm not bitter – life's too short for that. I just get sad."

The direct result of Girassol is that it drove Balmoral to merge its composites business with competitor (CRP Marine) to create Balmoral CRP. It need never have happened.

Renaissance?

Leaving aside bread and butter aspects of the group, such as its currently steady offshore mooring systems rental business, Balmoral has done a number of exciting things since the Girassol debacle, including diversifying into renewable energy, and has especially grown its tanks moulding division. This side of the business started in the mid-1990s with then Tory minister Michael Portillo giving the company a big thumbs up by agreeing to launch the operation.

Such huge numbers have since been manufactured that Balmoral tanks have become almost ubiquitous through the UK, both in the domestic and industrial markets. Until now, Aberdeen has been the centre of all manufacturing, but high transportation costs coupled with intense competition has driven Milne to start the search for a plant in the south. Most likely it will be located in Tamworth as the company already has a presence there. It is costing a 13% transport premium to get tanks shipped to the main markets in the English Midlands and South/Southeast. Given that 70% of output is sold south of Manchester, the cumulative impact of long-haul trucking is taking its toll on margins.

Bear in mind, the tanks business is now a core part of Milne's strategy to protect Balmoral against the vagaries of the oil and gas industry though, at the time of writing, he is locked in litigation over the failure of some tanks manufactured using sourced raw materials that may ultimately be proved defective. This is the so-called *Borealis* case.

He has also gone back to his roots by reviving composites (of which fibreglass is one) and started into alternative energy by manufacturing wind turbine nacelles for Vestas of Denmark, which has a turbine assembly business on the Scottish west coast.

"They did a fair in Glasgow designed to attract the interest of Scottish energy supply chain companies. I was dead chuffed because when they put up the nacelle contractor list there was only one company on it – Balmoral. I had heard they were coming so I took myself off to Denmark and convinced them we were the company to manufacture their nacelles in the UK. Fortunately for us, we had manufactured nacelles 20 years previously for Glasgow company Howden, which was first into the wind turbine business before selling out to the Continent."

But what of his people, tradesmen who have in many cases stuck by him through thick and thin?

"I'm blessed by having a heap of clever guys here at Balmoral and we all like a challenge. I'm sure that if this were a public company I would have been fired long ago because we never make money, but get a great deal of fun in what we're doing."

Milne qualifies for a free bus pass in December 2005, so what next?

"Most people in companies build them, sell up and retire in the sun somewhere. I'll never do that. I don't have holiday homes, or a yacht in the Mediterranean. I have a caravan up Deeside and I haven't seen it in a long time. I'm not envious.

"Watch this space!"

10 SIR IAN WOOD

MOGUL AMBASSADOR

SIR IAN WOOD

FACT FILE

Name	Sir Ian Wood
Company	John Wood Group PLC
Company turnover	£1.4 billion
Current position	Chairman & Chief Executive
Place of birth	Aberdeen
Education	Robert Gordon's College, Aberdeen, and University of Aberdeen
First job	Family fishing business
Best business decision	Every time I've chosen a really good senior colleague to join the team
Worst business decision	Lots of mistakes, most damaging of which are bad people choices. Fortunately, these have been few. The key is to admit you've made a mistake and correct it quickly
Which company in the upstream oil and gas industry industry do you admire and why?	There have been many significant players. History will record the North Sea story as an epic of technology and human achievement with many heroes, a few villains, many successes, a few failures, but most of all with a cast of unrelenting, committed and talented professionals dedicated to exploiting the UK's oil and gas reserves in a highly hostile deepsea environment
Biggest dislike of the industry	Our failure to manage the cyclicality. Our stop/start history is damaging, particularly to the attraction of the key talent which this very challenging and exciting industry requires
Advice to anyone considering a career in the oil industry	Don't be parochial – don't think Scotland, or UK, or even Europe. This is an increasingly global market. Travel and learn to understand the opportunities and threats of global markets
What do you think of management gurus?	Generally not much. Business is about some key commonsense principles and attracting and motivating the best people
Favourite pastime	Family, skiing, art and golf
Favourite book	The complete works of Robbie Burns
Who or what is your inspiration?	Wood Group's 14,000 employees across the world – I never fail to be delighted and inspired by their huge commitment, loyalty and extremely high quality skills
Any further ambitions?	Yes, many. In business I'd like to see Wood Group as one of the largest and most highly respected service companies in the oil and gas and power industries
Favourite quote/saying	Think global, act local

SIR IAN WOOD

MOGUL AMBASSADOR

Widely regarded as the doyen of the UK oil and gas supply chain, Aberdeen-born Wood Group chairman/CEO Ian Wood is a remarkable individual. Having initially read psychology at Aberdeen University he was diverted after graduation by family circumstance into business during the mid-1960s.

Today he is among Britain's wealthiest and leads a group that in 2004 turned over $2.25 billion, yet his was a reluctant corporate baptism into the world of business. Wood (many years later dubbed "Sir Ian" by the Queen) joined the family fishing and ship-repairing business, John Wood & Son, out of a sense of obligation as his father had fallen ill.

"I had a pretty healthy disrespect for the kind of pompous business style of that time," he recalls. "I was going through the process of being a young socialist, wanting to change the world, and had no intention whatsoever of going into the family business.

"I had wanted to become a doctor when I was a young guy. My uncle was a doctor in Tarbert, Harris and I spent every summer with him when I was 14 through 17 years old. He was one of my heroes. He was a very ordinary man who worked extraordinary hours, who would set off to see a patient, drive by car, take a boat trip, walk three miles to get to a lonely little but-and-ben in the middle of nowhere, never ever complained. He did it because that was his job, never got any recognition for it, except the whole community loved him. He was one of my heroes in the early days – not a business guy at all, but a fantastic man, a very simple man."

Like his father, the family firm was ailing and Sir Ian's mother was anxious about what the future might hold. So he had to help for a while at least and put his own career aspirations on hold. Ian Wood's father quite literally left him to run the firm and when he returned by degrees over a period of six months he concentrated on the shipbuilding side, leaving young Wood to deal with the fishing side of the business.

"He didn't even say get on with it. He just left me to do it."

What Wood rapidly discovered was how badly not only the family firm was being run but the whole fishing industry in Aberdeen at that time.

"It wasn't just John Wood & Son or the Don Fishing Company, but the whole industry, which was based on family businesses. It was business in the morning and gold in the afternoon."

So he set to work on the basis that, while lacking in experience, he at least had a trained mind. In any case, it rapidly became clear that it didn't take much imagination to get ahead of the field.

"Within two years we had put together a fleet of 12 vessels through acquisitions. However, these vessels originally fished individually with individual incentives. There was no incentive within the Wood fleet where, if a vessel got in among a lot of fish, to call in another unit.

"So we introduced a group incentive, also a secret code so fleet skippers could communicate securely with one another. To me it was such an obvious thing to do.

"Step back for a moment. I have an intense interest in people – in how you get the best out of them, how you create teams, how you motivate. And maybe this sort of action was an early manifestation of that. Trawler skippers are extraordinarily individualistic people and the only way to interest any of them at all was financially, that's why we introduced a fleet bonus system.

"And then people around the Aberdeen waterfront were asking: 'Why are the Wood vessels talking in code? What's going on?' Of course, within a year, every fleet had its own code."

A real driver for Wood was that he thought his sojourn with the business would be short – a few months, a year at most?

"I guess I was frustrated at having gone into the firm; part of me was saying I'm doing quite well and the business is expanding and the other kept telling me I was wasting my life."

The balancing factor for him was setting high personal goals each year to self-appraise against which, if he didn't get there, then he was not doing well enough. It was about pushing boundaries and it worked. By 1966–67 the fishing side of the business was back on its feet, three years after Wood left university in the summer of 1964. He describes the fishing industry of the late 1960s as static, parochial, a situation compounded by a languishing local economy. To help get things moving, he was trying to push the boundaries of the Wood business pretty hard.

The first acquisition came in 1966 – Aberdeen Motor Trawlers, which was a big bite to take. This was followed by the Minerva Fishing Company in 1967, which included fish processing. Wood had entered business puberty.

On the hook

"By the time I had done that I knew I was hooked because that was my responsibility. Previously I had taken on something that was my father's responsibility. When I had completed both of those takeovers I had way more than quadrupled the size of the business and you can't suddenly step away from that, not with so many people dependent on you."

Wood learned the need for good people early on and of the value of the team approach, which has been the bedrock of everything accomplished since. Moreover, this had to be done with care.

"Prior to this, there had been a very haphazard way of selecting people. But I spent a lot of time trying to get this right. I courted them, choosing individuals that competitors probably thought were beyond what they expected us to get. We really pushed the boat out by being prepared to pay a bit more. By 1968–69 we had achieved what I could describe as a management team that I could sit with and talk over issues."

Were these people who would challenge their young leader, perhaps pose a boardroom threat? He says some were, but that there was a caveat in the early days – the family.

"Remember, my family owned the business then, whereas Wood Group is a public company today. Back then the family was effectively all-powerful whereas with a public company you can be thrown out."

And what about the psychology used?

"From the beginning, I think, I gave people face. That's why I had to work at choosing good people and then try and give them space. Some have this image that, if you've done this, you must be autocratic. But I'm not autocratic. I make decisions at the end of the day, but I'm democratic to the extent that everyone is involved and consulted.

"I think I can still count on the fingers of one hand the times that I have said we will do this because I say so. If I've had to say that then I have failed – I've failed to get across the reasons why we should be going in such and such a direction.

"Right from the start, members of the team felt they were given space and were largely able to do what they wanted to do, though I was the final decision-maker.

"We introduced a share scheme too, in order to attract really good people. However, my father couldn't begin to understand why I would want to involve anyone else in the business.

"I was in my mid-20s, looked as though I knew what I was doing – but I was very young. Did I know what I was doing? Yes. I don't know what would have happened if oil hadn't come to Aberdeen, but I think we would have had a big fishing business.

"We were ambitious. We bought the shipyard John Lewis & Sons in 1971 – the Lewis lawyer insisted on getting a certified cheque because he didn't believe we could pay for the business. We borrowed money from the bank – we'd never done that before. With hindsight, buying that yard was a great move.

"We were lucky, the fishing, particularly off the Faroes in 1971–73, enjoyed three very reasonable years and generated the cash flow that gave us the confidence to buy John Lewis, also a bit of cash and breathing space to get into the oil industry.

"We worked very hard to create a good quality business; frankly it wasn't difficult to get ahead of the pack. Not that I saw that at the time; then I was frustrated and didn't know whether I was doing the right thing."

All the drive came from Wood junior as all his father was interested in was ship repairing. He declined to involve himself in fishing or, later, oil-related services.

Paying tribute to his father, who eventually died in 1985, Sir Ian says: "He was extraordinarily good and understanding, but he couldn't relate to what I was trying to do and didn't want to. There was never any friction, even in some of the difficult decisions we took."

In those days much of the firm's business was conducted using what would today be described as a bartering system – reciprocal trading of goods and services. It was a case of, you give me my ship repairing and I'll give you your oil, or trawl net repairs in return for, say, fish. But Wood decided this was outmoded and had to be stopped.

"I was unhappy at that. One of my father's long-term business associates was another major Aberdeen trawler owner. I thought the deal we had with them was totally in their favour and told him that I was going to have to change the arrangement. My father's reply was that they might take away the ship repairing. I acknowledged that they might but that we would be four times better off in terms of our getting a much better deal for oil.

"I eventually went head to head to deal with the issue. Father said he was uncomfortable, that he had been doing business with them a long time. I replied that I was not comfortable either. He didn't challenge me, he just commented that he wasn't comfortable. And then he didn't want to get involved.

"However, he supported me in terms of discussions with the bank when buying John Lewis & Sons, but I suspect he was less than comfortable but made no attempt to talk against it. I couldn't do that if I had my sons in the business. I'd be too keen to try and help and guide them! Mind you, my father enjoyed it. When there were various VIP visits he would come along."

Enter Big Oil

Young Wood had cut his teeth in an industry renowned for its toughness and one might have supposed that this go-ahead young Aberdonian felt well equipped to square up to Big Oil as it muscled its way in to the North Sea during the late 1960s and early 1970s. But he says he didn't see it that way at the time. An example: he had teamed up with the famous Edinburgh company Salvesen to bid for what was then called the South Bay base at Peterhead, 15 miles north of Aberdeen. They bid to the Scottish Office, which was promoting the idea. Wood and Salvesen were talking in terms of one rig and two supply vessels low case and perhaps four rigs and eight supply vessels at best. It was essentially a stab in the dark, the blind leading the blind, and they lost out.

"A guy called Jimmy Simpson came from absolutely nowhere, I guess offered twice as much as we did, the Scottish Office came back and said we should re-examine our bid. We did and said to Salvesen we couldn't go any higher, we're not prepared to take a bigger chance on this.

"Basically, we had no concept at all as to what this industry was about. Of course Jimmy Simpson won the bid. But it is very important to transport oneself back to these times and look at it from that perspective, not on the basis of the knowledge we have today. We thought we had a pretty aggressive approach to understanding what was happening and getting involved, without really knowing what it was all about.

"But I went to Houston in 1972 and my mind was completely blown by what I saw. I realised I had no idea what the oil industry was about. I hadn't the foggiest.

"It's too easy looking back and giving the impression that we knew what we were doing, we planned this and we planned that. We indeed did get together some good people, we had an early joint venture with the Weir Group, a couple of other false starts and joint ventures with people that wanted local content to get themselves into the North Sea game.

"But if you compared the quality of thinking and approach that you had at your disposal compared with a BP or Shell even in those days, it was entirely different from anything that Aberdeen had ever known. They were miles more professional."

Essentially, the greatest challenge was how to adapt and apply the existing skill-set to get a toehold in a far more demanding industry than fishing or ship repairing, learning on the hoof. No one had any idea how big it would become. But, even as early as the late 1960s, the view was that commercial fishing out of Aberdeen would be swamped and that there would be wholesale exploitation by Big Oil. And that really annoyed Wood.

"Alongside that, some of the early 'wildcat' exploration guys were patronising. They came to Aberdeen with the attitude that they could march in and walk over everyone; that local companies were to be used at their whim and that they were in control.

"Publicly I would say that we must get involved but, privately, I had no idea how we were going to do it. To be fair, in the beginning, the oil majors had some sympathy for local companies and encouraged us. But they didn't give us anything. However, we had the John Lewis yard and that gave us the basis of a mini-supply base in Aberdeen and that was probably the biggest single move we made in the early days that enabled us to get into the oil industry.

"When we bought the yard, we weren't sure what we'd do with it, but we knew that marine facilities were going to be key to this new industry. That was the time when Shell was persuading the city council to do away with historic old Torry village in order to build a base. That happened at the same time as we bought John Lewis."

Basically, Wood brought his top team together and discussed what the future might hold. It was still a fishing business, but they had to plot a course into the new future and that demanded careful thinking and strategising. And it seems that has never not been the Wood way throughout the 30-plus years of growing the Wood Group to what it is today, a company turning over $2.5 billion and employing 14,000 worldwide.

Essence of simplicity

"I've always sat down with the team and intellectually challenged ourselves and thought through the strategy. We didn't use the word in the early days, but looked at various alternatives, risks and, without ever having any kind of sophisticated analysis, we actually did the things you should do.

"That's why I often say to business school students, business is actually very basic – it's a very simple process. Much of it is instinctive. It is a thinking process where people are extraordinarily important in the equation and where you simply think through the basics. It's not complicated at all, which is why I don't like complicated business books.

"Business books will make it miles more complex than it really is. The biggest thing they don't get across at business school is the importance of people. They'll tell you all the different issues that you're involved in. But they won't get across the fact that nothing will happen without people working together.

"The trickiest thing I do and have done since I first started in business is to get people together in their thinking, whether employees, customers or whoever, to get them pointed in the direction they need to go.

"In terms of developing teams today, by far the most important thing I do is choose people in terms of internal promotion or external appointments and get them settled in and pointed in the right direction. And contrary to what you might think, I'm not a high-profile guy. Instinctively, I'm not. I enjoy being with my colleagues, I enjoy travelling around seeing the group businesses, enjoy the process of business itself, but I don't really enjoy the limelight.

"Wood Group inevitably gained a profile early because we were among the most successful of UK companies to engage with oil and gas, but that's not something I ever attached any importance to."

However, Sir Ian did flirt with glamour at least in his 20s and 30s and especially as his involvement with oil gathered momentum and the service firm that he established at the start of the 1970s, the embryonic Wood Group, became recognised.

"I definitely took a position on BRIT, the British indigenous technology drive, which was a government initiative designed to push UK industry to maximise the opportunity presented by the North Sea. I picked up that flag very early on."

When Margaret Thatcher came to power as UK prime minister, Sir Ian learned to play the political hand, engaging with ministers like Alick Buchanan-Smith and Peter Walker.

In the late 1980s/early 1990s especially, Wood was again to use his growing profile to good effect in the campaign to get oil-related civil servants to Aberdeen. This was a game that was to a great extent played out in the media, especially *The Press and Journal*.

"But I'm not an easy wicket," insists Wood. "I will do it but it's not something I enjoy doing."

People person

He might not like being in the limelight, but Sir Ian is a people person. Indeed this is central to his ethos.

"This company is people. Without them it doesn't happen and yet there are individuals out there who are really bad with others.

"As you travel the world like I do, the people skills become even more important because you face entirely different cultures – fundamentally different ways of thinking. Your ability to try and understand your own emotions and motivations and control and direct them in the right way in dealing with that becomes incredibly important.

"Here in Aberdeen, what I've been saying to Aberdeen Business School (Sir Ian is currently chancellor of the Robert Gordon University) lately is that, as well as teaching basic business, as the global economy advances we must increasingly teach how one does business around the world."

He says that approaches that sell Wood Group services and technology in the UK or US apply perhaps 45–50% internationally. The rest is accessible only by understanding how business is done elsewhere and it has nothing to do with corruption, which Wood ranks about number six in terms of challenges.

"It's fundamentally about understanding the nature of the people, nature of relationships and all the issues that go into the Arab world, or the Russian world, or the Chinese world. Take Russia – a command economy until 15 years ago. They fundamentally think differently about the nature of business and employing people.

"Globalisation is the biggest single change over the span of my life time. When I went into business I could afford to have a UK mindset and perspective and I could be successful. But, in the world we live in now, almost every business you're in you cannot have a local perspective. You've got to understand the nature of trading across the world, skills across the world, and it requires a different mindset. Unfortunately, it's one of the things Scotland is still furthest behind in. We still have a mindset whereby England is regarded as the competition. It should be the world.

"You know there are two million engineering graduates in China per annum. The world is changing at an incredible pace."

While Wood has become a multi-cultural human being, many others cannot hack it. By and large, it seems that he has been able to trickle that spirit through much of his company. The accent chimes with the mantra of Percy Barnevik of ABB fame – "think global act local".

As far as Wood is concerned, Schlumberger is the ultimate in oil and service companies as has a thoroughly global workforce. As for Wood Group, he says it is much more international than five or ten years ago.

"But it doesn't come by altering Brits or Americans. It comes by genuinely having a group of people who come from all the cultures and who you try and meet fairly regularly and ensure through some process of osmosis that there is understanding."

Servant leader

But how does Wood hold the whole thing together; after all, Brits can be very conservative, narrow-minded people? Essentially it's all about distributed manage-ment – comprehensive delegation.

"Wood Group ceased to be me beginning 15 years ago. There is an extremely able bunch of guys out there, some based here, some in the States, others elsewhere, who are the prime movers of the group. I'm a servant leader (a term adopted from the excellent management book *Good to Great* by Jim Collins). My role is to ensure that the key guys at the top are the right guys, to do some coaching, counselling, seldom directing, go around and attend quarterly review meetings: (a) to be seen and (b) to meet people and see what's going on.

"Wood Group is no longer me. If I disappeared tomorrow I guess there would be a process of adjustment and change, but the excellent people who are there now will continue to be there. I would count it as a major failure on my part if the company stumbles after I'm gone. Handing over the reins is clearly partly there. I have five – six key colleagues. They largely make the decisions and execute them. I'm the servant leader. However, at the end of the day I'm still the guy who, with very difficult decisions, sits down with them and the rest of the board and we make them."

Wood is dismissive of the widely held notion that he is a brand in his own right. "You've missed a trick if you still think it's me. The media thinks that way.

"Great companies are not led by outstanding personalities who demand a high public profile and who are continually introducing new strategies and publicly say this, that and what have you. They are led by fairly quiet guys who have been in the organisation for a long time, have generally come from within, have a fairly low profile, are very driven and develop a really strong team about them."

This is almost a direct take from *Good to Great*, which is one of very few management books that Wood will have truck with.

"Why I like the book is that I empathise with the way they see a company should be run. One of my strengths is that I'm certainly not over-confident. I doubt, but I'm not under-confident. Along with my colleagues, I'm continually re-examining and this is in sharp focus right now as Wood Group has endured a very difficult two years and we've made a number of important changes. We've grown our revenues in each of the last two years, but we had flat profits in 2003 and a reduction in profits last year."

Wood insists on shouldering the blame for the mistakes that led to this poor performance.

"I was aware of what was going on. The buck stops at me if we get it wrong. But you can't turn a thing like that around overnight, not with the size of the company. We try desperately hard to be a whole lot of small to medium-sized companies that can think and act fast. We really try to cut out politics and inertia, but it inevitably appears."

And growth remains firmly on the agenda.

"We haven't got anywhere near where we're going to finish up. Today is just part of a growing process. You keep looking for the next horizon and the one after. Then you wake up in the morning to see whether you've done it. I don't feel I've done it. That's the honest truth. I've got to a certain stage but there's a whole range of challenges out there.

"Yes, my role is very different now to what it was ten years ago," says Wood Group's chairman. "But letting go is difficult. It's made easier by the fact that the group is now so large.

"I'm in my international phase right now. I'm also doing the PILOT and ILT thing (these are two UK oil industry initiatives) and I was chairman of Scottish Enterprise for three years, which was partly about giving my colleagues space two days a week.

"The world and the media may still see Sir Ian Wood as the Wood Group but they're absolutely wrong. I may still play a key role, but 80% of key decisions are made without me. The most important ones I'm aware of, I ain't making them, others are."

Sense of responsibility

As if he doesn't already have enough on his plate, Wood feels a duty to fight for the wider UK oil and gas industry, its potential and its shortcomings. He is particularly critical of government short-sightedness and says more, much more, needs to be done to assure the future of Britain's most successful industry since 1945, one that has pumped nearly £200 billion of taxes and royalties into treasury coffers.

"I feel this huge sense of responsibility. I suppose it's a bit of a burden. I do it because I'm one of the leading players in Aberdeen and an Aberdonian; I want to be judged by the next generation, hopefully, as someone who was aware of the issues and tried to do something. It's now about how that next generation will judge how we handled the oil boom and what we got out of it long term.

"Is it going to finish by 2030, 2040, or 2050, that's one key issue; and, secondly, are we really going to have an international base here?"

He is hopeful that this might indeed come about as more UK supply chain companies are doing international business than in the past. Ten years ago, when Wood chaired the government's Offshore Supplies Office, if 15–20% of companies were doing international business, that was good. It is now more than 50%.

Nonetheless, he is deeply worried that there are people in government and elsewhere who have failed to understand the value of the oil and gas industry to the UK as a strategic and international trade asset. The North Sea could still be worth a staggering £560 billion to Britain if the right effort is made.

"But the attitude is worse than that. Some think that it is over now. You wouldn't believe how strongly I feel about this. I meet serious people in government who actually think the North Sea oil story is largely over. That's one thing.

"Secondly, they don't give a damn about the northeast of Scotland or Scotland, so the issue that we try and establish a long-term, international industry from here doesn't enter their minds. Why should they even bother making that connection? All they're worried about is the impact of oil on the UK economy – the balance of payments. Many see North Sea oil as just that.

"But that's fair because that's what I would expect. What we need to do is make enough noise, fuss and bother to ensure they actually realise there are different dimensions to all of this. I've spent the last year-and-a-half to two years inside the North Sea industry's PILOT steering group, really strongly leading this concept of maximising recoverable reserves.

"Crusade? I suppose it is. I really don't want people to look back on this period and judge it as entirely selfish, that people just took advantage of it, made the money they could, but with no really long-term thought.

"It sounds corny, my grandfather and seven brothers were fishermen in Aberdeen. I don't want to destroy the community that has effectively given them this opportunity. That would be a massive failure.

"If Wood Group was a big, successful company that remained successful internationally, yet the northeast of Scotland had slumped into recession in 10, 15, 20 years' time, I would feel that we had handled it very badly. So there's the crusade, to ensure the North Sea leads to real lasting value for Scotland and the northeast.

"Nobody else cares about that. Everyone else is worrying about their particular part of the UK, or industry. We have to manage it. People make the mistake of thinking that somehow it is government's role to do it. It isn't."

Paradox

Wood pointed out that when Aberdeen's main thoroughfare, Union Street, was built in the late 1800s it almost bankrupted the city, yet was probably what made it. What he feels today is that his birthplace is a very enterprising city to the extent that there are a lot of businesses, a lot of young business people who really are pretty aggressive, enterprising, committed, hardworking, keen.

"This is a whole new, much more professional and dynamic business community than we've ever had. This isn't the family businesses of the fishing industry; this is much different. But, you know, we haven't had the kind of spark of what I would call massive collective enterprise – working together to actually take Aberdeen to the next level.

"It's happened in the harbour – sustained heavy investment has resulted in a very modern port, albeit very dependent on the oil industry. But we haven't 'done the Union Street'. We haven't got the legacy that people in 50 years' time will look back and say, that's what the oil industry gave us – tangible, clear, massive.

"When I was chairing Grampian Enterprise, I saw the revamp of Union Terrace Gardens as one thing that might have a huge impact. It's that scale of enterprise that's lacking. It might still come."

And so back to people.

"It's about people – careful thinking, planning, analysis – decisions that look easy only seem so because a huge amount of work has been done behind them; and the other thing you must always do is admit it when you get something wrong. Far too many people in business charge on and either don't see that they've got it wrong or somehow try and hide from it. One of the best decisions you can make in business is to reverse a bad decision."

THE MAKING OF THE MOGULS

This section is about trying to draw together some of the common and divergent themes of the ten profiles that form the core of this book. As already explained, the decision was taken at the outset to let the individuals tell their own stories in the belief that this is the best way for the reader to gain some insight into how they tick and address the huge challenges and opportunities presented by the upstream oil and gas industry, especially offshore.

In *Energy*, a monthly supplement to Aberdeen's *The Press and Journal* newspaper, there is a regular series called "From the Boardroom" – interviews with leading lights of the upstream oil and gas industry. The objective of these features is both to entertain and inform. What is particularly memorable about the series from the author's perspective as editor is just how diverse these individuals are. They cover a huge spectrum ranging from oil company CEOs to those who lead large service corporations on both sides of the Atlantic. They represent a mix of company men and self-made individuals – entrepreneurs, if you prefer.

While a fair proportion of the 30 or so senior figures to submit to the "From the Boardroom" process over the period March 2003 through July 2005 doubtless fit broad stereotypes, most do not. Many are plain maverick, and perhaps that's what makes them so fascinating and why oil and gas leadership is worth studying in its own right, as it is an industry that still possesses a huge pioneering spirit.

The *raison d'être* for "From the Boardroom", as with this book, is that if the reader can garner from the material ideas that they can apply to their business, life in general, or studies, then it will have succeeded. I firmly believe in the process of learning from others, whether directly, via the written word or some other way. It is something that none of us should ever stop doing. When interviewing Sir Ian Wood for this book, I was intrigued when he produced a well-thumbed copy of *Good to Great* by Jim Collins. And it really was much used – peppered as it was with pencilled notes and underlining. This is a man, at the pinnacle of his profession, seeking to learn from others. However, Wood is also a man who has no time for conventional business books whereas the quirkiness and simplicity of *Good to Great* chimes absolutely.

The UK oil and gas community looks up to Sir Ian. While he has for the past 15 years regarded himself as a "servant leader" within the company that he founded – the John Wood Group, others in the industry see him as perhaps the number one leader within the indigenous British energy supply chain – a man of wisdom, someone to learn from, the automatic choice for high-level North Sea and Department of Trade and Industry/UK Trade and Investment committees/initiatives.

The stock market is less sure about his skills. Since the company listed, it has failed to live up to expectations, with some shareholders latterly baying for blood. While results for the past few years have indeed been nowhere near as good as they ought to have been, one reason why the market is unsure about the Wood Group is that most analysts don't understand its structure, or rather they haven't made a real effort to learn what it is. In essence it is a quasi-federation of small to medium-sized business units gathered together under a common banner but in a totally different way to the famous ABB matrix created by Percy Barnevik.

Wood talks of an organisation made up of silos: he deliberately uses this term, even though it often has negative connotations attached.

"I like to think we're not the same as ABB," he says. "We try to achieve the best of both worlds – decentralise yet be related to teams of people who are empowered with responsibility but then know their own silo. They know how they relate to the structure, they're empowered, they know what their objectives are, they know what their incentives are. The model works."

Wood says there are two key issues: "One is the degree of synergy between those silos, and we have a lot of that; moreover, it has increased over the past four or five years. Secondly, how do you incentivise these, let's say, 10 football teams, each with its own manager, own bit of culture and what have you; how do you incentivise them to play the Wood Group game? That's probably where we've made most progress in the past five years. We have a lot more mini-conferences, really getting people talking to one another more."

It's all about communications with a view to learning.

Incidentally, the only member of the sample group obviously to have a business book to hand during the interviews was Jim Atack, in his case *Up the Organisation* by Robert Townsend. He also confessed to loving Dilbert and, let's face it, which boss worth his or her salt could not extract something from this cartoon character.

Common heritage

One of the most striking aspects to emerge from talking to the 13 individuals concerned – four of them brothers – was common heritage, the most obvious being that 11 are engineers of one form or another. The odd ones out are Wood, with his degree in psychology, and Oilexco's founder/president Arthur Millholland, who is a geologist. Most chose not to go to university, either for family background reasons or because they simply wanted to get out and earn a wage.

The counterpoint to 11 being trained engineers is that only one pursued business studies at the outset, but to diploma, not degree level. That was AMEC's Neil Bruce. All other formal business qualifications – and then only Bruce and Vetco International's chairman John Kennedy – were gained in later life. Bruce read for an MBA at University of Newcastle and Kennedy notched up an MSc in Finance at The London Polytechnic.

Stepping back even further, five started their lives on the farm, so to speak – the four Dreelan brothers on the parental farm in Co. Wexford, Ireland, and Jimmy Milne, who was born only a few hundred yards from the headquarters of the company he founded and runs today – Balmoral Group. Both the Dreelans and Milnes were large families, with their respective siblings developing a work ethic and an ability to co-operate at an early age.

Interestingly, neither the Dreelan brothers nor Milne went to university from school, mostly preferring to leave the classroom early and get a job. Just one Dreelan went to college. Yet, all ended up training as engineers, in Milne's case as an agricultural engineer. Two of the Dreelans started out as heating and ventilation engineers and one became a time-served carpenter! None of the foregoing five have had any formal management training during their subsequent careers, with the exception of short courses.

In oil career terms, five started off at Schlumberger – three of the Dreelans, John Kennedy and Larry Kinch all acquitted themselves as specialists in well service engineering. Each received high quality training and had to go through periodic refreshers, which is one of the hallmarks of Schlumberger. In professional terms it is hard to get off to a better start in oilfield life than to work for a corporation of this standing; and the North Sea SME community is liberally sprinkled with former Schlumberger engineers that eventually made a break for freedom, leaving behind comfortable careers.

Sharp contrasts

The contrasts between the Schlumberger five are sharp indeed. Only one joined this energy service blue chip as a university graduate – Kennedy, who then went on to reach the top, in industry supply chain terms, as a Halliburton VP. Only then did Kennedy take the entrepreneurial road, but by invitation rather than because he was hacked off as an employee. In both cases – Wellstream and Vetco International – he has taken the chair of large businesses with a significant track record and then applied his considerable expertise.

In a sense, Kinch is Kennedy's opposite – left school early, became an engineering apprentice at a paper mill, took his chance by applying for a job with Schlumberger, worked his way up, switched across to an oil company (Shell) but became restless in his early thirties. Since then, Kinch has gone on to create not one, or two, but three successful businesses, each very different. The first is Petroleum Engineering Services that was eventually sold to Halliburton for more than £100 million, the second is the now listed UK oil independent Venture Production, and the newest is the currently unique hybrid Energy Development Partners that in mid-2005 was applying the finishing touches to the UK's first energy investment fund.

Other than Milne, if anyone in this study fits the description serial entrepreneur, then it is surely Kinch, though he self-effacingly dismisses the notion that he is any such thing.

Petrofac's Jim Atack made, perhaps, the most unpromising and latest start of any of the group, having left school early with little idea of what he wanted to do with his life. It took several years of working in the tough world of building sites and motorway construction before Atack focused and then rapidly realised his latent potential as an engineer, storming through University of Loughborough and then on to MIT to read for his Masters before joining BP.

In contrast, Bruce was quick off the mark in terms of joining the industry having left school early, then going to college in Dundee to do a business studies diploma. He then joined Brown & Root, since when he has turned in an excellent performance, largely as a company man. Like Kinch, he was raised in Aberdeen, which was already coming under heavy North Sea influence during his formative years, so making the offshore industry choice was almost inevitable.

Another company man is Tom Ehret. As he says in his profile Ehret landed in the oil and gas industry quite by chance. Had there not been a delay to his being called up for national service in France, this son of Alsace with a degree in engineering might not have given the industry a single thought. Happenstance saw him take a temporary job at the then already famous French underwater technology company Comex. The rest is history, so to speak. Ehret has achieved in the underwater contracting sphere what Kennedy did in oil services *per se*, except that Ehret's stage has largely been Europe, whereas many of Kennedy's successes have been played out in the US. But, unlike the Irishman, Ehret did not avail himself of the opportunity to read for a Masters. Innate ability, coupled with excellent mentoring and not a few boardroom storms along the way, have got him to where he is today – CEO of Stolt Offshore, one of Europe's (and the world's) largest and most influential subsea contracting firms.

At the opposite end of the subsea spectrum to Ehret is Richard Marsh, founder and managing director of Tritech International, a Scottish SME that commands the lion's share of a niche underwater technologies market worth around £10 million a year.

Marsh also found his way into the oil and gas sector by chance. This aeronautics engineer is a member of the team that built the world's only commercial supersonic airliner – Concorde. The switch came only at the end of the Concorde construction programme when Marsh was given the opportunity to get involved in remotely operated vehicle technology development. It was only much later that he hit the entrepreneurial trail by first setting up a company called Bennico using Norwegian money, and later, in 1990, Tritech International from largely his own resources.

Marsh is an oddball and utterly passionate about engineering, moreover, British engineering. In some ways he has created the quintessential small British business insofar as Tritech has always been and, for so long as he is involved, always will be at the 'S' end of SME. But that is where the similarity ends. That Tritech has attracted two Queen's Awards and the Royal Society of Edinburgh Millennium prize, plus multiple Scottish Offshore Achievement Awards demonstrates that the Marsh strategy has worked. He has created a very special business and such performance has, of course, attracted interest from the financial community and would-be suitors, but all have been rebuffed.

Marsh's company is living proof that small can be beautiful in the corporate world. Moreover, there is the distinct danger that what has been created might be destroyed if a venture capital provider, for example, took a stake because of the risk of conflicting financial outlooks. This comes through very clearly in comments such as: "Making money is probably eighth or tenth on the list of things that make me happy. I've no more interest in making money."

Succession

Marsh's biggest problem is succession. He says he is enjoying a fabulous retirement – it's called Tritech – but admits that there is no obvious successor in the frame, either family or member of staff/minor shareholder. This has to be a dilemma, though the question is shrugged off with a chuckle.

Jimmy Milne is arguably in the same situation, only different. Balmoral is a much bigger enterprise and his style is totally different. And yet he possesses much the same madly inventive, have a go, streak that is such a characteristic of the cultivated Marsh.

Milne has been to hell and back several times in his long career as a businessman: witness the crash of a prior company, Aberglen, the deep crisis precipitated at Balmoral by a $50 million contract to manufacture sophisticated deepwater buoyancy systems for the Girassol oilfield development off West Africa, and the current (mid-2005) battle over materials used to manufacture water tanks that were found to be defective.

Step back to the mid-1990s and Milne also thought he had the succession issue under control as his much younger brother-in-law, Mark Patterson, was then involved in a senior role. But disagreements put an end to that and Milne, who graduates to a bus pass at the end of 2005, has no obvious successor. This too is laughed off. In his case the response is: "Most people in companies build them, sell up and retire in the sun somewhere. I'll never do that."

Wood believes he has the succession issue at Wood Group well covered and that has been the situation for some time. To reiterate:

"It's happening, absolutely happening," he insists. "There are lots of things going on in Wood Group now that I'm not involved with but was 10 years ago. Handing over the reins is clearly partly there. I have five – six key colleagues. They largely make the decisions and execute them ... The world and the media may still see Sir Ian Wood as the Wood Group but they're absolutely wrong. I may still play a key role, but 80% of key decisions are made without me. The most important ones I'm aware of, I ain't making them, others are."

Succession is not an issue for any of the other subjects, either because they are corporate men and will be ousted over time anyway (this includes Kennedy as a stock exchange listing for Vetco International is in the near-term strategy); or it is not yet relevant.

The Dreelans have their solution in place in that Tommy (the eldest) sees Ciaran (the youngest) as his natural successor. This is helped by a 17-year gap between their birth dates.

"We've never talked about it directly, what we make sure is that this business can run without one of us tomorrow. You cannot run a business around one person," says the senior Dreelan.

Valuing people

All the subjects in this study appear to understand very clearly that, without the support of skilled workforces and colleagues, they are as nothing. Each has a different way of handling this most fundamental of corporate issues and it is clear that it also generates emotion, especially with Marsh and Milne – Marsh because he was recently subjected to low-level fraud that betrayed the immense trust which he places in the Tritech team; and Milne because of the way so many of the Balmoral workforce have stood loyally by him through thick and thin.

Whereas Milne is very traditional in his approach and, being the son of a farmer, is from a similar background to many of the Balmoral stalwarts, Marsh gained first-hand knowledge of the impact that arrogant, ignorant handling can have on a workforce during his Concorde years.

"I had joined British Aerospace as a right wing Tory pratt and one who thought that unions were the devil's creation because that's what I was told. After six months there I had total sympathy for trade unions.

"Over those 12 years, that company taught me everything I ever needed to know about how *not* to treat people."

That he has obviously been hurt by the Tritech low-level incident will do nothing to change his basic, very humanistic approach to his staff. But it is now tempered by that souring experience.

The Dreelans are very conscious of the people issue, both from the perspective of board composition and the need to ensure that all staff are thoroughly trained and kept in the picture. The boardroom aspect is particularly important given the strong family content.

"We've avoided the pitfall of filling the Qserv boardroom with brothers. We don't run it as a family business because, to attract the right people to work for us, the right calibre of management, it is very important that we are all seen as individuals. We just happen to be brothers, we just happen to be shareholders. We want everyone to be open and honest and avoid the brothers ganging together thing where people feel excluded."

For Sir Ian, it has never not been people, right from his earliest days when propelled into the family's ailing and traditional commercial fishing and ship repair business. It comes through time and again that this canny Scot doesn't just talk the talk; he very much walks the walk when it comes to caring for and valuing staff. The author knows a number of Wood Group employees who love him deeply. Given the size of the company today, with 14,000 employees across the globe, it is quite remarkable that one individual can engender such emotions in an industry as cut throat as oil and gas.

There is a curious similarity between Sir Ian and Bruce in that both talk with a quiet passion about their people and genuinely mean it. Like Wood, this aspect of Bruce comes through time and again, from the way he engages with the "shop floor", to graduates, to his top-team.

An excellent illustration of this can be seen in the way he turned around safety performance at AMEC's offshore fabrication complex on Tyneside. Bruce says the formula was simple. He took a personal interest and tried to get out on-site every day, unless he was away. It was about getting the hard hat on and going around the yard and chatting with the lads – hundreds, even a thousand and more tradesmen – on a virtually one-to-one basis.

"To begin with I was viewed fairly sceptically, but I think that, after showing face day after day, week after week, month after month, a genuine interest started to develop," he recalls.

And management: "One thing I firmly believe in is having a team of mixed capabilities and strengths and getting them to spark off against one another."

Perhaps at greatest risk of becoming distanced from his people has been Kennedy by virtue of his meteoric climb coupled with excellent academic provenance. It is potentially a recipe for remoteness but what has perhaps helped him avoid that pitfall is that he is Irish and there are few better communicators anywhere. This may be a politically incorrect view to adopt, but that's the way Kennedy comes across and the many other Irish people that the author has encountered, even in Siberia.

The following statement says a lot about Kennedy: "I always look upon business as, this is not the army, it's an elective situation. If you don't treat people properly they don't have to stay around. They can leave. So you have to make it worth their while professionally and personally to stay with you."

And what about Arthur Millholland, who has been building a team in Aberdeen in order to pursue his North Sea dream? This highly individualistic, straight-talking Canadian is in no doubt that he cannot do it alone and counts himself incredibly lucky to have secured the talent that now works out of Oilexco's modest offices.

It's about having the right people – doing something simple and getting it done," says the geologist.

"We've been lucky. We've found some very good people here; we've met them over the past three years. They're people with a light shining from within. Some really talented people have even come and asked whether they can join us."

And later: "I can't do everything. We're hiring good people and we trust them."

Finally on people, there is the Atack style. Once again, like Bruce, like Wood, we have a quiet, unassuming individual at the head of a large workforce and who has that indefinable something about him that makes him a leader of people. I'm not at all sure that he really knows where it comes from, though he says that road construction and building sites, and being only five feet eight inches tall, made it abundantly clear that he couldn't play the tough guy with workers who were taller, broader and physically more together than he was, even if he had wanted to.

Diplomacy was the only way forward if he was to be a leader and that has stuck. And perhaps it really is that simple; we often look for highly complex reasons behind a particular behaviour or action when the answer is blindingly obvious – and simple. Given the heavy emphasis on people at Petrofac, such a skill is essential for successful leadership, not that Atack pushes the subject.

"I'm not sure that I intend for people to buy-in to me as an independent leader; I hope I have a shared vision with enough people so that most of us say: 'These are the things we're trying to do.' There's a clear understanding, it makes sense, and people are then motivated to follow that lead. It's not a single leader issue for me."

Conclusion

One of the characteristics of most, if not all, of the individuals, without whom this book would never have been written, is their role within the wider community, particularly energy-related. And easily the biggest surprise was sprung by Arthur Millholland for his role in the UN Oil for Food programme in Iraq.

Successful people almost invariably take on wider roles. In the business context two exemplars are Sir Ian Wood, who has done an enormous amount to fight for the UK oil and gas industry, and Richard Marsh, who is a leading light within the Subsea UK initiative designed to highlight what is a high-value, technologically advanced aspect of British industry.

In community/social issues terms, Jimmy Milne has done an incredible amount to highlight the plight of cancer sufferers, while Jim Atack is responsible for Petrofac's pioneering and enduring relationship with a senior school located in one of Aberdeen's less well-off districts – Kincorth. None shout about it; they just want to help. All defy the classic imagery of hard-bitten businessmen riding roughshod over both employees and the wider community, dispensing largesse only when it suits their political ends.

Where they are all hard-bitten, however, is fighting for the future of the UK's upstream oil and gas capability. The North Sea is past half-time in terms of its commercially viable lifespan, with perhaps 20–30 billion barrels oil equivalent left to be extracted, and much of that has yet to be located. Actually securing this incredible prize will require every technological trick and business model in the book, and many that have not yet been invented. But that's just the UK domestic prize. It is important to realise that the North Sea is just one part of the largest and wealthiest industry on the planet, with all forecasts pointing to trillions of dollars being invested in new projects and maintaining existing production capability.

The race is on to find and exploit vast quantities of oil and gas, and the clock is ticking. Pressure on available resources is mounting rapidly and oil has been in the headlines almost every day since the start of 2005, with prices getting just past $60 per barrel compared with less than $10 per barrel during late 1998. And, in the UK, gas prices have been as high as $80 per barrel oil equivalent in 2005.

All this points to unprecedented opportunities for the upstream oil and gas capability that has grown up during the 35 or so years since a meaningful North Sea industry started to emerge. It is the author's view that this should have been a rehearsal for a brilliant long-term global future for this tremendous energy capability. And yet, over the period late 1977 through 1999, an incredible 100,000 jobs were shed from the UK's upstream capability, leaving roughly 260,000 jobs, of which around one-third are located in Scotland. This massive attrition has been brought about by oil companies seeking to drive down costs at every level; and the result today is that, with prices soaring and domestic output falling, there are signs of panic setting in. Skills shortages across the board are endemic with little fresh blood coming into the industry as it has wrecked its own previously good reputation.

Companies in the supply chain are increasingly at full stretch, their capabilities having been sliced to the bone because of the way in which their clients (the oil companies) have behaved in recent years. And yet I can't help thinking that it will somehow all come "right" in the end.

Forty years ago there was no North Sea oil and gas industry. Today there is. Forty years ago, except for oil companies like BP, there was a minimal indigenous capability geared to international markets; today there is a huge capability geared to both the domestic and international market.

Essentially, a powerful industry was grown from scratch in less than 40 years; and at no time has there not been a skills crisis of one form or another. That is the normal state in any sector, especially one as cyclical as oil and gas.

And what about the leadership? One of the remarkable aspects of the North Sea industry has been the way in which competitors have been willing to work together for mutual benefit, especially during a time of crisis, even if it doesn't seem that way much of the time. The author knows of no other sector of the British economy where this happens so comprehensively. Aberdeen is the only city in Britain where you will regularly get 200–400 industry leaders coming together for a working breakfast to chew over issues – and they're oilmen.

The average age in the UK oil and gas industry is now 53 – and that's about the average age of our sample. While this obviously gives cause for huge concern, what must not be overlooked is that there is at least a decade in hand for that generation to pass on its skills and for many of the big issues, such as recruitment, to be resolved. And with energy coming to the fore in the way it is, that has to be a source of comfort.

But what a pity it is that so very few women have made it into the UK's offshore industry, let alone made a mark thus far. Indeed, the only UK woman to smash through the glass ceiling is Belfast-born Alison Goligher, a senior VP at Schlumberger

Perhaps the coming decades offer an opportunity to redress this huge imbalance in this rather chauvinistic industry.

It was said at the outset that this book would be simple. One could continue the analysis of this tiny cross-section of energy moguls almost *ad infinitum*, including how they approach the thorny subject of strategy and business plans – the Dreelans didn't have these for years. But I'm going to end here, except to say that I believe they characterise this incredible "telephone numbers" industry.

And there are hundreds, if not thousands, more like them out there. The 13 profiled herein are simply a taste of that talent.

JEREMY CRESSWELL

BIOGRAPHICAL NOTE

Jeremy Cresswell is an energy journalist/analyst who specialises in upstream oil & gas and renewables. He writes primarily for Britain's oldest daily newspaper, *The Press and Journal* of Aberdeen which he joined in November 1989. In addition, he contributes to many other business and energy-oriented titles and has co-authored a significant number of reports and publications including Scottish Enterprise energy annuals, 1997–2001 and Mackay Consultants reports, notably World Offshore Oil & Gas Report, 2004–2008; Mediterranean & Black Sea Oil & Gas Report, 2004–2008; and Americas Report, 2004–2008.

Cresswell carried out ground-breaking research into the potential impact of offshore oil & gas on the Faroese business community while reading for his MBA at Aberdeen Business School in the mid 1990s. He instigated the successful 'All Energy' conference series staged in Aberdeen since 2001 and, at the invitation of Aberdeen City Council, initiated the private-public partnership Aberdeen Renewable Energy Group of which he is chairman. In 2001, Cresswell was co-opted onto the Scottish Enterprise Grampian working party that drew up the successful North-east bid for Scotland's new Energy Intermediate Technology Institute based in Aberdeen.

Conversations with North Sea Oil Moguls is Cresswell's third book. He has also written *Black Gold and the Silver City* – a history of the Balmoral Group/diary of North Sea oil - and, *Tide and Time*, a history of the Craig Group.

MATTHEW R. SIMMONS

BIOGRAPHICAL NOTE

Matthew Simmons is Chairman and Chief Executive Officer of Simmons & Company International, a specialised energy investment banking firm. The firm has completed approximately 600 investment banking projects for its worldwide energy clients at a combined dollar value in excess of $65 billion.

Simmons was raised in Kaysville, Utah. He graduated *cum laude* from the University of Utah and received an MBA with Distinction from Harvard Business School. He served on the faculty of Harvard Business School as a Research Associate for two years and was a Doctoral Candidate.

Simmons serves on the Board of Dean's Advisors of Harvard Business School and is a past President of the Harvard Business School Alumni Association and a former member of the Visiting Committee of Harvard Business School. He is a member of the Council on Foreign Relations and The Atlantic Council of the United States.

His recently published book *Twilight in the Desert: The Coming Saudi Oil Shock and the World Economy* has been listed on the Wall Street Journal's best-seller list. He has also published numerous energy papers for industry journals and is a frequent speaker at government forums, energy symposiums and in board rooms of many leading energy companies around the world.